FREE VIDEO  **FREE VIDEO**

Essential Test Tips Video from Trivium Test Prep!

Dear Customer,

Thank you for purchasing from Trivium Test Prep! We're honored to help you prepare for your exam.

To show our appreciation, we're offering a **FREE *Essential Test Tips* Video by Trivium Test Prep.*** Our video includes 35 test preparation strategies that will make you successful on your big exam. All we ask is that you email us your feedback and describe your experience with our product. Amazing, awful, or just so-so: we want to hear what you have to say!

To receive your **FREE *Essential Test Tips* Video**, please email us at 5star@triviumtestprep.com. Include "Free 5 Star" in the subject line and the following information in your email:

1. The title of the product you purchased.

2. Your rating from 1 – 5 (with 5 being the best).

3. Your feedback about the product, including how our materials helped you meet your goals and ways in which we can improve our products.

4. Your full name and shipping address so we can send your **FREE *Essential Test Tips* Video**.

If you have any questions or concerns please feel free to contact us directly at: 5star@ triviumtestprep.com.

Thank you!

– Trivium Test Prep Team

*To get access to the free video please email us at 5star@triviumtestprep.com, and please follow the instructions above.

Civil Service Exam Study Guide 2021–2022

PREPARATION BOOK WITH PRACTICE TEST QUESTIONS
FOR THE CIVIL SERVICE EXAMS (POLICE OFFICER,
FIREFIGHTER, CLERICAL, AND MORE)

ELISSA SIMON

Copyright © 2021 by Trivium Test Prep

ISBN-13: 9781635308877

ALL RIGHTS RESERVED. By purchase of this book, you have been licensed one copy for personal use only. No part of this work may be reproduced, redistributed, or used in any form or by any means without prior written permission of the publisher and copyright owner. Trivium Test Prep; Accepted, Inc.; Cirrus Test Prep; and Ascencia Test Prep are all imprints of Trivium Test Prep, LLC.

Trivium Test Prep is not affiliated with or endorsed by any testing organization and does not own or claim ownership of any trademarks. All test names (and their acronyms) are trademarks of their respective owners. This study guide is for general information and does not claim endorsement by any third party.

Printed in the United States of America.

TABLE OF CONTENTS

INTRODUCTION i

1 READING 1

The Main Idea 1

Supporting Details....................................2

Drawing Conclusions 3

The Author's Purpose
and Point of View..............................4

Comparing Passages....................6

Text Features............................7

Types of Sources 9

Meanings of Words........................10

Following Directions and
Recognizing Sequences 11

Interpreting Verbal and
Graphic Communications 13

Answer Key 15

2 WRITING 17

Grammar....................................17

Capitalization 23

Homophones and Spelling..............24

Sentence Structure..........................26

Answer Key 30

**3 VERBAL AND
REASONING SKILLS** 33

Vocabulary....................................33

Synonyms and Antonyms 38

Analogies 39

Visual Analogies and Sequences........39

Answer Key 42

4 MATHEMATICS 43

The Most Common Mistakes 43

Strategies for the
Mathematics Section 43

Numbers and Operations 44

Algebra 54

Statistics and Geometry 58

Answer Key 61

5 CLERICAL SKILLS 75

Alphabetization 75

Alphabetization and
Filing Questions 78

Speed and Accuracy 80

Communication and Judgment 82

Memorization................................83

6 PRACTICE TEST 85

Reading 85

Verbal Ability................................91

Mathematics 102

Clerical Skills................................105

Answer Key 125

INTRODUCTION

Congratulations on choosing to take the next step in your career by preparing for your civil service exam! By purchasing this book, you've taken an important step on your path to becoming a civil servant in a municipality, state, or the United States federal government.

This guide will provide you with a detailed overview of the content covered on most civil service exams, so you will know exactly what to expect on exam day. We'll take you through all the important concepts and give you the opportunity to test your knowledge with practice questions. Even if it's been a while since you last took a major exam, don't worry; we'll make sure you're more than ready!

WHAT IS THE CIVIL SERVICE EXAM?

Local and state governments and the United States federal government all need qualified personnel at every level. To this end, they use comprehensive exams to assess candidates. There are several types of civil service exams administered to candidates. The exam or exams you take depends on the position you apply for. Exams are varied. They measure candidates' reading, writing, and reasoning abilities. Some exams also test mathematical skills. A variety of exams test clerical ability.

WHAT'S ON THE CIVIL SERVICE EXAMS?

The type of civil service exam you take depends on the job you apply for. Different exams test different subjects. Still, there are a few major topics covered on almost every exam. Candidates may be evaluated on their reading, language, mathematics, and clerical skills. Some tests may have only a few questions and take a short time. Others may have up to one hundred multiple-choice questions and be approximately two hours long. The number of questions and exact time vary by test. Again, it all depends on the job for which you apply.

The bottom line is, there is no one single civil service exam: different exams exist for different jobs. This book offers a review of the most common types of questions found on most civil service exams.

Reading Questions

READING questions test your ability to understand written texts, analyze the information presented, and draw conclusions. You will be asked to identify the main idea, details, and/or draw conclusions from reading passages. You may also be asked about vocabulary. You do not need to use outside information for these questions.

Verbal Skills Questions

Verbal skills questions test your grammatical and **WRITING** skills. You may be asked about subject-verb agreement, spelling, or sentence structure. Some questions ask you to complete a sentence by choosing the correct word; other questions ask you to choose the clearest of several sentences. You may also be asked to improve the draft of a passage, fixing errors in usage and grammar, or determining clarity and efficacy of writing.

Many exams test **SPELLING** skills. You might be asked to identify the correct spelling of a word. Exams may also test your **VOCABULARY**, asking you to choose the synonym or best definition of a word.

Finally, some civil service exams feature **ANALOGIES**. These may be verbal or visual, and they test your reasoning abilities.

Mathematics Questions

Depending on the job you are applying to, you may be asked to solve some **MATHEMATICS** problems. Civil service math exams are generally straightforward and involve simple arithmetic; however, there may be more complex questions concerning fractions, decimals, ratios, or proportions. In rare cases, you may encounter basic algebra. This book provides a review of all these concepts.

Clerical Questions

Some civil service exams feature clerical questions, especially for candidates applying to administrative positions. This book provides an in-depth discussion of clerical skills as well as two practice clerical tests that contain questions you are likely to see on the exam.

ALPHABETIZATION questions test your ability to quickly and accurately file names in alphabetical order. **CODING** and **COMPARISON** questions evaluate your attention to detail by asking you to compare names or addresses and search for errors, or to determine the accuracy of a numerical code. **MEMORIZATION** questions test your observation skills. You will have two minutes to review a photograph or picture; then you will be asked questions about details in the image.

Not every civil service exam contains each kind of clerical question, but this book provides practice for the most important and common question types.

ADMINISTRATION AND TEST DAY

Different civil service exams are administered by participating agencies. In some cases, you may be asked to take the exam online from your home as part of the application process and promise not to use any outside assistance. It is important to understand that you are on your honor to do your best with no outside help. In other cases, you may test at a facility.

To register for an exam, you must directly contact the participating agency where you are applying. Most exams will be administered in either a pencil-and-paper or computer-based format. Check with your agency to be sure.

Arrive early on test day. Check with the facility or participating agency to make sure you know what type of identification to bring (usually government-issued photo identification). Bring at least two sharpened No. 2 pencils. Personal belongings, cell phones, and other electronic, photographic, recording, or listening devices are not permitted in the testing center. Many testing centers offer lockers to secure your personal items, but you should check beforehand with the facility to be sure storage is available.

TIPS FOR TACKLING MULTIPLE-CHOICE QUESTIONS

The following tips assume you have a basic understanding of test-taking: how to follow test proctor instructions, how to properly record answers, making sure the answer for the right question is recorded, and reviewing your answer sheet before submitting it. If you do nothing else to prepare, learn these quick tips—they will help you focus your efforts and use your time wisely.

Handling Distractors

DISTRACTORS are the incorrect answer choices in a multiple-choice question. They "distract" you from the correct answer. Read and answer the question below:

Criminals are people who violate _____.

A) Penal Code 62

B) civil procedure

C) martial law

D) criminal laws

The correct answer choice is D) criminal laws. The other, incorrect answer choices—the distractors—are designed to distract the inattentive test taker by "sounding" right or formal. While choices A and C may be partially correct—breaking a specific penal code (criminal) or martial (civilian-imposed military) law may be a crime—neither is the best answer choice.

Be sure to read the question for context and tone, and try to determine what is being asked. The preceding question asks for a general definition and uses wording from the question as part of the correct answer. While a criminal might violate a specific penal code or martial law, generally, violations can be of any criminal law. Because criminals are guilty of crimes and all criminal laws involve or pertain to crime, choice D is the best answer.

Develop a Time Strategy

Most civil service exams are around two hours long. Pay attention to the time: note the start and end time for each section prior to beginning, and make a goal to complete each question in one minute or less. One minute seems like a short amount of time, but it actually is not. You will likely complete most questions in less than thirty seconds. Develop your strategy such that you finish the easier questions quickly, allowing more time to focus on the difficult questions.

Don't spend too much time on difficult questions; instead, mark them, skip them, and come back when you have time.

Focus on the Question

Read the question carefully. Words sometimes change meaning based on context. Context is the part of communication that comes before or after a specific word or passage and provides clarity or meaning. Make sure you read and understand the question before selecting an answer. Read the following sentences:

> The police **<u>arrested</u>** Chad when he was eighteen years old.
>
> Chad is thirty-two years old, but his emotional development was **<u>arrested</u>** when he was eighteen years old.

The word *arrested* is used correctly in both sentences, but it has different meanings depending on the context.

Try to think of an answer before looking at the choices. This can keep you from being distracted by the incorrect choices and help you more easily identify the correct answer.

Correct is Not Always Best

Several answers could be correct, or close to correct, but you must choose the best answer choice. Beware of answer choices that are close to the correct answer but are merely distractions.

Use the Process of Elimination

Eliminate answer choices you know are incorrect; choose your answer from the remaining choices.

For "all of the above" and "none of the above" answer choices, look for options that include elements that break the "all" or "none" rule, such as a true element in a group of false elements or vice versa. If one element does not belong with the rest of the group's elements, then the answer cannot be all, or none, of the above.

Reread the question and remaining answers and select an answer choice.

ABOUT THIS GUIDE

This guide will help you master the most important test topics and develop critical test-taking skills. We have built features into our books to prepare you for your exam and increase your score. Along with a detailed summary of the test's format, content, and scoring, we offer an in-depth overview of the content knowledge required to pass the test. Throughout the guide, you'll find sidebars that provide interesting information, highlight key concepts, and review content so that you can solidify your understanding. You can also test your knowledge with sample questions throughout the text as well as practice questions. We're pleased you've chosen Trivium to be a part of your journey!

READING

THE MAIN IDEA

The **TOPIC** is a word or short phrase that explains what a passage is about. The **MAIN IDEA** is a complete sentence that explains what the author is trying to say about the topic. Generally, the **TOPIC SENTENCE** is the first (or near the first) sentence in a paragraph. It is a general statement that introduces the topic so that the reader knows what to expect.

The **SUMMARY SENTENCE**, on the other hand, frequently (but not always!) comes at the end of a paragraph or passage because it wraps up all the ideas presented. This sentence summarizes what an author has said about the topic. Some passages, particularly short ones, will not include a summary sentence.

QUICK REVIEW

To find the main idea, identify the topic and then ask, "What is the author trying to tell me about the topic?"

Table 1.1. Identifying Topic and Main Idea

The cisco, a foot-long freshwater fish native to the Great Lakes, once thrived throughout the basin but had virtually disappeared by the 1950s. However, today fishermen are pulling them up by the net-load in Lake Michigan and Lake Ontario. It is highly unusual for a native species to revive, and the reason for the cisco's reemergence is even more unlikely. The cisco have an invasive species—quagga mussels—to thank for their return. Quagga mussels depleted nutrients in the lakes, harming other species highly dependent on these nutrients. Cisco, however, thrive in low-nutrient environments. As other species—many of which were invasive—diminished, cisco flourished in their place.

TOPIC SENTENCE	The cisco, a foot-long freshwater fish native to the Great Lakes, once thrived throughout the basin but had virtually disappeared by the 1950s.
TOPIC	cisco
SUMMARY SENTENCE	As other species—many of which were invasive—diminished, cisco flourished in their place.
MAIN IDEA	Cisco had nearly disappeared from the lake, but now flourish thanks to the invasive quagga mussel.

Examples

Tourists flock to Yellowstone National Park each year to view the geysers that bubble and erupt throughout it. What most of these tourists do not know is that these geysers are formed by a caldera—a hot crater in the earth's crust—which was created by a series of three eruptions of an ancient super volcano. These eruptions, which began 2.1 million years ago, spewed between 1,000 to 2,450 cubic kilometers of volcanic matter at such a rate that the volcano's magma chamber collapsed, creating the craters.

1. What is the topic of the passage?

A) tourists

B) geysers

C) volcanic eruptions

D) super volcanos

The Battle of Little Bighorn, commonly called Custer's Last Stand, was a battle between the Lakota, the Northern Cheyenne, the Arapaho, and the Seventh Cavalry Regiment of the US Army. Led by war leaders Crazy Horse and Chief Gall and the religious leader Sitting Bull, the allied tribes of the Plains Indians decisively defeated their US foes. Two hundred and sixty-eight US soldiers were killed, including General George Armstrong Custer, two of his brothers, his nephew, his brother-in-law, and six Indian scouts.

2. What is the main idea of this passage?

A) Most of General Custer's family died in the Battle of Little Bighorn.

B) The Seventh Cavalry regiment was formed to fight Native American tribes.

C) Sitting Bull and George Custer were fierce enemies.

D) The Battle of Little Bighorn was a significant victory for the Plains Indians.

SUPPORTING DETAILS

Statements that describe or explain the main idea are SUPPORTING DETAILS. Supporting details are often found after the topic sentence. They support the main idea through examples, descriptions, and explanations.

> **HELPFUL HINT**
>
> To find supporting details, look for sentences that connect to the main idea and tell more about it.

Authors may add details to support their argument or claim. FACTS are details that point to truths, while OPINIONS are based on personal beliefs or judgments. To differentiate between fact and opinion, look for statements that express feelings, attitudes, or beliefs that can't be proven (opinions) and statements that can be proven (facts).

Table 1.2. Supporting Details and Fact and Opinion

Bait is an important element of fishing. Some people use live bait, such as worms and night crawlers. Others use artificial bait, such as lures and spinners. Live bait has a scent that fish are drawn to. Live bait is a good choice for fishing. It's cheap and easy to find. Lures can vibrate, make noise, and mimic the movements of some fish. People should choose artificial bait over live bait because it can be used multiple times.

SUPPORTING DETAILS	Lures can vibrate, make noise, and mimic the movements of some fish.
FACT	Live bait has a scent that fish are drawn to.
OPINION	Live bait is a good choice for fishing.

Examples

Increasingly, companies are turning to subcontracting services rather than hiring full-time employees. This provides companies with advantages like greater flexibility, reduced legal responsibility to employees, and lower possibility of unionization within the company. However, this has led to increasing confusion and uncertainty over the legal definition of employment. Courts have grappled with questions about the hiring company's responsibility in maintaining fair labor practices. Companies argue that they delegate that authority to subcontractors, while unions and other worker advocate groups argue that companies still have a legal obligation to the workers who contribute to their business.

3. Which detail BEST supports the idea that contracting employees is beneficial to companies?

    A) Uncertainty over the legal definition of employment increases.

    B) Companies still have a legal obligation to contractors.

    C) There is a lower possibility of unionization within the company.

    D) Contractors, not companies, control fair labor practices.

Chalk is a colorful way for kids and adults to have fun and be creative. Chalk is used on playgrounds and sidewalks. Children love to draw pictures in different colors. The designs are beautiful, but they are also messy. Chalk doesn't clean up easily. It has to wash away. Chalk is also used by cafés and bakeries. Shops use chalk to showcase their menus and special items. It is a great way to advertise their food.

4. Which statement from the passage is an opinion?

    A) It is a great way to advertise their food.

    B) Chalk doesn't clean up easily.

    C) It has to wash away.

    D) Shops use chalk to showcase their menus and special items.

DRAWING CONCLUSIONS

Readers can use information that is EXPLICIT, or clearly stated, along with information that is IMPLICIT, or indirect, to make inferences and DRAW CONCLUSIONS. Readers can determine meaning from what is implied by using details, context clues, and prior knowledge. When answering questions, consider what is known from personal experiences and make note of all information the author has provided before drawing a conclusion.

HELPFUL HINT

Look for facts, character actions and dialogue, how each sentence connects to the topic, and the author's reasoning for an argument when drawing conclusions.

Table 1.3. Drawing Conclusions

When the Spanish-American War broke out in 1898, the US Army was small and understaffed. President William McKinley called for 1,250 volunteers to serve in the First US Volunteer Cavalry. The ranks were quickly filled by cowboys, gold prospectors, hunters, gamblers, Native Americans, veterans, police officers, and college students looking for an adventure. The officer corps was composed of veterans of previous wars. With more volunteers than it could accept, the army set high standards: all the recruits had to be skilled on horseback and with guns. Consequently, they became known as the Rough Riders.

QUESTION	Why are the volunteers named Rough Riders?
EXPLICIT INFORMATION	different people volunteered, men were looking for adventure, recruits had to be extremely skilled on horseback and with guns due to a glut of volunteers
IMPLICIT INFORMATION	Men had previous occupations, officer corps veterans worked with volunteers.
CONCLUSION DRAWN	The men were called Rough Riders because they were inexperienced yet particularly enthusiastic to help with the war and were willing to put in extra effort to join.

Example

After World War I, political and social forces pushed for a return to normalcy in the United States. The result was disengagement from the larger world and increased focus on American economic growth and personal enjoyment. Caught in the middle were American writers, raised on the values of the prewar world and frustrated with what they viewed as the superficiality and materialism of postwar American culture. Many of them fled to Paris, where they became known as the "lost generation," creating a trove of literary works criticizing their home culture and delving into their own feelings of alienation.

5. Which conclusion about the effects of war is most likely true?

   A) War served as an inspiration for literary works.

   B) It was difficult to stabilize countries after war occurred.

   C) Writers were torn between supporting war and their own ideals.

   D) Individual responsibility and global awareness declined after the war.

THE AUTHOR'S PURPOSE AND POINT OF VIEW

The **AUTHOR'S PURPOSE** is an author's reason for writing a text. Authors may write to share an experience, entertain, persuade, or inform readers. This can be done through persuasive, expository, and narrative writing.

PERSUASIVE WRITING influences the actions and thoughts of readers. Authors state an opinion, then provide reasons that support the opinion. **EXPOSITORY WRITING** outlines and explains steps in a process. Authors focus on a sequence of events. **NARRATIVE WRITING** tells a story. Authors include a setting, plot, characters, problem, and solution in the text.

STUDY TIP
Use the acronym *P.I.E.S.*— *persuade, inform, entertain, state*—to help you remember elements of an author's purpose.

Authors also share their POINT OF VIEW (perspectives, attitudes, and beliefs) with readers. Identify the author's point of view by word choice, details, descriptions, and characters' actions. The author's attitude or TONE can be found in word choice that conveys feelings or stance on a topic.

TEXT STRUCTURE is the way the author organizes a text. A text can be organized to show problem and solution, comparison and contrast, or even cause and effect. Structure of a text can give insight into an author's purpose and point of view. If a text is organized to pose an argument or advertise a product, it can be considered persuasive. The author's point of view will be revealed in how thoughts and opinions are expressed in the text.

Table 1.4. The Author's Purpose and Point of View

Superfoods are foods that are found in nature. They contain rich nutrients and are low in calories. Many people are concerned about healthy diets and weight loss, so superfoods are a great meal choice! Rich antioxidants and vitamins found in superfoods decrease the risk of diseases and aid in heart health.

AUTHOR'S PURPOSE	persuade readers of the benefit of superfoods
POINT OF VIEW	advocates superfoods as "a great meal choice"
TONE	positive, encouraging, pointing out the benefits of superfoods, using positive words like *great* and *rich*
STRUCTURE	cause and effect to show use of superfoods and results

Examples

University of California, Berkeley, researchers decided to tackle an age-old problem: why shoelaces come untied. They recorded the shoelaces of a volunteer walking on a treadmill by attaching devices to record the acceleration, or g-force, experienced by the knot. The results were surprising. A shoelace knot experiences more g-force from a person walking than any rollercoaster can generate. However, if the person simply stomped or swung their feet—the two movements that make up a walker's stride—the g-force was not enough to undo the knots.

6. What is the purpose of this passage?

    A) to confirm if shoelaces always come undone

    B) to compare the force of treadmills and rollercoasters

    C) to persuade readers to tie their shoes tighter

    D) to describe the results of an experiment on shoelaces

What do you do with plastic bottles? Do you throw them away, or do you recycle or reuse them? As landfills continue to fill up, there will eventually be no place to put our trash. If you recycle or reuse bottles, you will help reduce waste and turn something old into a creative masterpiece!

7. Which of the following BEST describes what the author believes?

    A) Landfills are unnecessary.

    B) Reusing objects requires creativity.

    C) Recycling helps the environment.

    D) Reusing objects is better than recycling.

Negative cinematic representations of gorillas have provoked fear and contribute to hunting practices that endanger gorilla populations. It's a shame that many films portray them as scary and aggressive creatures. Their size and features should not be cause for alarm. Gorillas are actually shy and act aggressively only when provoked.

8. What can be inferred about the author's attitude toward gorillas?

A) The author is surprised that people do not know the truth about gorillas.

B) The author is concerned that movies distort people's opinion of gorillas.

C) The author is saddened by the decrease in gorilla populations.

D) The author is afraid that gorillas are being provoked.

Want smoother skin? Try *Face Lace*, a mix of shea butter and coconut oil. Like most creams it is soft and easy to apply. We rank #1 in sales and free trials. Our competitor *Smooth Moves* may be great for blemishes, but we excel at reducing the signs of aging!

9. What is the structure of this text?

A) cause and effect

B) order and sequence

C) problem and solution

D) compare and contrast

COMPARING PASSAGES

Sometimes readers need to compare and contrast two texts. After reading and identifying the main idea of each text, look for similarities and differences in the main idea, details, claims, evidence, characters, and so on.

HELPFUL HINT

Use a Venn diagram, table, or highlighters to organize similarities and differences between texts.

When answering questions about two texts, first identify whether the question is about a similarity or a difference. Then look for specific details in the text that connect to the answers. After that, determine which answer choice best describes the similarity or difference.

Table 1.5. Comparing Passages

APPLE CIDER VINEGAR

Apple cider vinegar has many medicinal properties. It is used for cleaning and disinfecting. When ingested, it lowers blood sugar levels, increasing insulin function and fighting diabetes. Studies are being conducted to determine if it can aid in shrinking tumors and cancer cells, and lower the risk of heart disease.

ALKALINE WATER

Many people believe that alkaline water increases immune system support; prevents cancer; and aids in antiaging, detoxification, and weight loss. Unfortunately, having an excess amount of alkaline water in the body could produce nausea, vomiting, and tremors.

SIMILARITIES (COMPARISON)	Both substances are ingested and used to fight diseases.
DIFFERENCES (CONTRAST)	Alkaline water has negative side effects, whereas apple cider vinegar is being studied to prove its usefulness.

Example

PANDA BEARS

Panda bears live in China's bamboo forests. They eat bamboo and are excellent tree climbers. New roads and railroads break the flow of the forest, isolating panda populations. This decreases the amount of food pandas can access during the year.

POLAR BEARS

Polar bears live in the Arctic and are the largest land carnivores in the world. They eat seals and walruses. As the sea gets larger from melting ice, polar bears have to travel longer distances for food. Their thick white fur provides warmth and traction for their feet on the ice. They are good swimmers.

10. Which of these statements BEST compares the information in both texts?

   A) A carnivore's diet depends on animals in the area.

   B) The destruction of habitats affects food supply.

   C) Animals must be able to move easily in their environment.

   D) An animal's population can change its habitat.

TEXT FEATURES

TEXT FEATURES are components of a text that include information that is not in the main text. They help readers determine what is essential in a text and show where to find key information. Before reading, look at the text features to get an understanding of what a text is about.

HEADINGS and SUBHEADINGS show how information is organized and help readers identify the main points of each section in a text.

FOOTNOTES are notes at the bottom of a page that reference or cite information, definitions, explanations, or comments.

Text features such as ITALICS and BOLDFACE are used for emphasis. Italicized words appear slanted and signify titles, scientific terms, footnote references, and emphasized words. Boldface print makes words stand out from the rest of the text on a page and draws the reader's attention. It highlights ideas, to introduce new vocabulary, or to emphasize main points.

Text features that help to organize information are the TABLE OF CONTENTS and INDEX. The table of contents shows a book's structure, outlining its sections and chapters. An index consists of a list of words and phrases in alphabetical

HELPFUL HINT

Text features help readers increase background knowledge and learn new information.

order that outlines various topics in a book. Page numbers are provided to guide readers to sections of the book.

Table 1.6. Text Features

CHAPTER TWO: RATTLESNAKES

RATTLESNAKE HABITATS

There are 13 species (*crotalus* or *sistrurus*) of rattlesnakes. Rattlesnakes adapt to different **habitats**. They can live in deserts, meadows, or swamps. Rocky crevices are great places to hide and make dens.

KEEPING PREDATORS AWAY

Rattlesnakes have a rattle at the base of their tails. The vibrations of the rattle deter **predators**. Hissing sounds are also a warning to other animals[1]. Other ways to ward off predators include coiling their bodies and raising their heads in order to strike and bite.

[1] Some rattlesnakes camouflage themselves to avoid predators.

BOLDING	habitats, predators
ITALICS	crotalus, sistrurus
HEADING/ SUBHEADING	Chapter Two: Rattlesnakes/Rattlesnake Habitats, Keeping Predators Away
FOOTNOTE	Some rattlesnakes camouflage themselves to avoid predators.

Examples

INDEX

B
basic operation 7
battery 7

C
call log 9
cell phone 7
contacts 9
cordless phones 6

D
delete information 9
dialing numbers 9

H
handset 10

I
installation 7
Internet 8

L
landline 5

M
memory card 8

P
pay phone 6

R
receiver 5
ringtone 9
rotary phone 5

S
SIM card 9
smart phone 7

T
text message 10
touch screen 9

V
voicemail 10

W
Wi-Fi 8
wireless network 8

11. What inference can be made about this book based on its index?
    A) The book is about different types of phones.
    B) The book is about modern-day mobile phones.
    C) The book is about the history of cell phones.
    D) The book is about how to contact someone via phone.

Popular stories like *The Three Little Pigs* are often retold and changed into what are known as *twisted* fairy tales. *The Three Little Javelinas* is a similar tale to *The Three Little Pigs*, but it has a different setting and characters. It takes place in a desert instead of a forest, and the javelinas outsmart a coyote instead of a wolf.

12. Italics are used in the text to indicate which of the following?

A) titles and references to footnotes

B) foreign phrases

C) emphasized words and titles

D) scientific terms

TYPES OF SOURCES

Researching a topic is easier if you know the types of information sources available to you.

PRIMARY SOURCES consist of original material and text, providing a firsthand account of events. Some examples of primary sources are diaries, photographs, records, interviews, eyewitness accounts, autobiographies, and recordings.

SECONDARY SOURCES are materials and text often created after the events have taken place. They are used to analyze and support primary sources. Examples of secondary sources include biographies, encyclopedias, textbooks, and articles.

TERTIARY SOURCES are sources that compile, organize, and summarize other sources. They are used to locate primary and secondary sources and provide a brief overview of the topics and information from these sources. Examples of tertiary sources include indexes, abstracts, bibliographies, directories, almanacs, handbooks, and databases.

HELPFUL HINT
To determine which source you are using, think about whether the information on the topic serves as direct evidence or supporting evidence of events.

Table 1.7. Types of Sources

Nick is planning a report on Amelia Earhart. After searching for information, he has the following sources: document index, photographs, journal articles, biographies, video clips, encyclopedia entries, newspaper articles, and digital archives.

PRIMARY SOURCES	photographs, newspaper articles, and video clips
SECONDARY SOURCES	encyclopedia entries, biographies, and journal articles
TERTIARY SOURCES	document index and digital archives

Example

Alexander Hamilton and James Madison called for the Constitutional Convention to write a constitution as the foundation of a stronger federal government. Madison and other Federalists like John Adams believed in separation of powers, republicanism, and a strong federal government. Despite the separation of powers that would be provided for in the US Constitution, anti-Federalists like Thomas Jefferson called for even more limitations on the power of the federal government.

13. Which sources would be MOST useful for a book report on this event?

   A) indexes, diaries, and photographs
   B) surveys, interviews, and databases
   C) abstracts, almanacs, and textbooks
   D) encyclopedias, articles, and biographies

MEANINGS OF WORDS

To understand the meanings of unfamiliar words in a passage, use CONTEXT CLUES. Context clues are hints the author provides to help readers define difficult words. They can be found in words or phrases in the same sentence or in a neighboring sentence. Look for synonyms, antonyms, definitions, examples, and explanations in the text to determine the meaning of the unfamiliar word.

Sometimes parts of a word can make its meaning easier to determine. AFFIXES are added to ROOT WORDS (a word's basic form) to modify meaning. PREFIXES are added to the beginning of root words, while SUFFIXES are added to the ending. Divide words into parts, finding meaning in each part. Take, for example, the word *unjustifiable*: the prefix is *un–* (not), the root word is *justify* (to prove reasonable), and the suffix is *–able* (referring to a quality).

Another way to determine the meaning of unknown words is to consider their denotation and connotation with other words in the sentence. DENOTATION is the literal meaning of a word, while CONNOTATION is the positive or negative associations of a word.

Authors use words to convey thoughts, but the meaning may be different from a literal meaning of the words. This is called FIGURATIVE LANGUAGE. Types of figurative language include similes, metaphors, hyperboles, and personification.

Similes compare two things that are not alike with the words *like* or *as*. Metaphors are used to compare two things that are not exactly alike but may share a certain characteristic.

Hyperboles are statements that exaggerate something in order to make a point or draw attention to a certain feature. Personification involves using human characteristics to describe an animal or object.

HELPFUL HINT

Use what you know about a word to figure out its meaning, then look for clues in the sentence or paragraph.

Table 1.8. Meanings of Words

Have you ever gone to a flea market? There are rows of furniture, clothing, and antiques waiting for discovery. Unlike a museum with items on display, flea markets are opportunities to learn and shop. Vendors bring their handmade goods to this communal event to show their crafts and make money.

CONTEXT CLUES	Vendors are people who sell things; people shop at a flea market.
AFFIXES	The prefix *com–* in *communal* means *with* or *together*.
MEANING	*Communal* means "shared with a community."

Examples

The Bastille, Paris's famous historical prison, was originally built in 1370 as a fortification—called a *bastide* in Old French—to protect the city from English invasion. It rose 100 feet into the air, had eight towers, and was surrounded by a moat more than eighty feet wide. In the seventeenth century, the government **converted** the fortress into an elite prison for upper-class felons, political disruptors, and spies.

14. Which word or phrase can be used to determine the meaning of *converted*?

    A) originally built

    B) fortification

    C) felons

    D) historical prison

Breaking a world record is no easy feat. An application and video submission of an amazing skill may not be enough. Potential record breakers may need to demonstrate their skill in front of an official world records judge. The judge will watch a performance of a record attempt to determine if the record-breaking claim is **credible**. After all evidence is collected, reviewed, and approved, a certificate for the new world record is granted!

15. Based on affixes and context clues, what does *credible* mean?

    A) believable

    B) achievable

    C) likeable

    D) noticeable

Every year people gather in Durham Park to participate in the Food Truck Rodeo. A band plays, and the food trucks are like a carnival of delicious treats. The aroma of food draws all who pass by, creating a large crowd. The event is free to attend; patrons pay only for what they want to eat. From pizzas and burgers to hot dogs and pastries, there's something for everyone!

16. Which type of figurative language is used in the second sentence?

    A) hyperbole

    B) metaphor

    C) personification

    D) simile

FOLLOWING DIRECTIONS AND RECOGNIZING SEQUENCES

When following a set of directions, look for SIGNAL WORDS that indicate steps of a process. These words will tell you when things need to happen in a certain order. Signal words should show a transition from one event or step to another.

When reading a passage, you will find that signal words can be used to follow the direction of the author's ideas and the sequence of events. Signal words show time order and how details flow in a chronological way.

HELPFUL HINT

To find signal words, ask, "What happened first and what happened after that?"

Table 1.9. Following Directions and Recognizing Sequences

NASA wanted to launch a man from Earth to the moon. At first they used satellites for launch tests. Then in June of 1968, astronauts aboard the Apollo 8 launched into space and circled the moon ten times before returning to Earth. Finally, in 1969 three astronauts reached the moon in the Apollo 11 spacecraft. After a successful landing, two members of the crew walked on the moon. During their walk they collected data and samples of rocks. They returned as heroes of space exploration.

SIGNAL WORDS	At first, Then, Finally, After, During

Examples

FANTASTIC HARD-BOILED EGGS

Ingredients
6 eggs

Steps
Place the eggs at the bottom of a saucepan.

Fill the saucepan with enough water to cover the eggs.

Heat the saucepan on high heat until the water comes to a boil.

After the water comes to a boil, turn it down to medium heat and continue boiling for 8 minutes.

Strain the water from the pan and run cold water over the eggs to cool them.

Peel the eggs under a little running water.

Serve.

17. According to the recipe, which action should be completed first?

   A) Peel eggs under water.

   B) Fill the saucepan with water.

   C) Heat the water to a boil.

   D) Strain the water from the pan.

Babies learn to move their bodies over time. Head control is first developed at two months to create strong neck, back, and tummy muscles. Next, the abilities to reach, grasp, and sit up with support happen around four to six months. By the end of six months, babies learn to roll over. After six to nine months, babies can sit on their own and crawl. During age nine to twelve months, pulling and standing up are mastered. Finally, after gaining good balance, babies take their first steps!

18. Which BEST describes the order of a baby's movement over time?

   A) roll over, control head, sit up, crawl

   B) sit up, roll over, crawl, walk

   C) control head, reach, crawl, roll over

   D) sit up, grasp, crawl, walk

INTERPRETING VERBAL AND GRAPHIC COMMUNICATIONS

Verbal communications can be used to send a message or information to an individual or a group. Memos, advertisements, and flyers are all ways in which ideas and information can be shared. Key elements include the heading, subject, date, message, pictures, and a call to action (information telling readers how to respond).

To better understand what is written, try to identify the author's intention and the purpose of the text. The structure of the text will help clarify the main points. Important parts may be presented in paragraphs, bullet points, or bold print.

Graphic communications are used to locate places, identify parts of an object, and demonstrate processes. Key parts include graphics, labels, numerical data, colors, symbols, and lines that show direction, connections, or relationships among parts.

Table 1.10. Interpreting Verbal and Graphic Communications

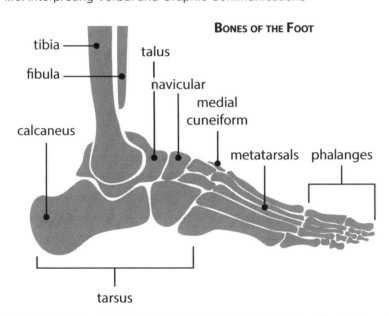

HEADING	Bones of the Foot
PICTURE	visual representation of the parts of the foot
LINES/BRACKETS	outlining sections of the foot and the relationships between them
LABELS	providing the name of each part of the foot

Examples

To: All Employees
From: Dennis Frazier, Manager
Date: 08/28/17
Re: Email Communication

This is a reminder of our Email Policy.

1. Please refrain from sending company-related emails through personal email accounts. Use company-assigned email accounts for all correspondence.

2. Please email managers and team leaders about time off at least three days in advance. Last-minute emails or phone calls are not acceptable.

3. Please respond to emails within forty-eight hours, as some are time-sensitive.

Thank you in advance for helping us all work better together!

19. Which best describes the writer's purpose?

    A) to ensure that all employees use email properly

    B) to persuade employees to use email more

    C) to show appreciation for employees working together

    D) to inform all employees of a new email policy

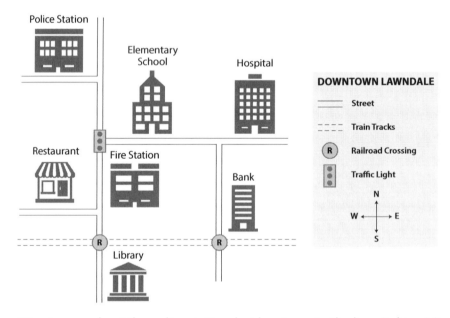

20. Jean works at the police station, but has to go to the hospital to visit a friend. If she goes to the library before she goes to the bank, and only walks on streets, avoiding the train tracks, how many times will she pass by the Lawndale traffic light?

    A) 2

    B) 3

    C) 4

    D) 5

ANSWER KEY

1. **B)** The topic of the passage is geysers. Tourists, volcanic eruptions, and super volcanos are all mentioned in the explanation of what geysers are and how they are formed.

2. **D)** The author writes that "the allied tribes...decisively defeated their US foes," and the remainder of the passage provides details to support this idea.

3. **C)** The passage specifically presents this detail as one of the advantages of subcontracting services.

4. **A)** The statement "It is a great way to advertise their food" is a judgment about how the shops use chalk to show menu items to customers. The word *great* expresses a feeling, and the idea cannot be proven.

5. **D)** After the war, there was a lack of focus on the world and greater focus on personal comforts, which writers viewed as superficiality and materialism.

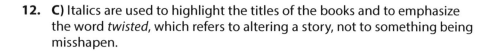

6. **D)** The text provides details on the experiment as well as its results.

7. **C)** The author states that recycling and reusing objects reduce waste, which helps the environment.

8. **B)** The author demonstrates disapproval of film portrayals of gorillas and how they influence people's views of gorillas.

9. **D)** In this text, two brands of cream are being compared and contrasted.

10. **B)** Both passages indicate that habitats are diminishing, impacting access to food.

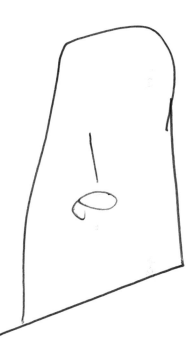

11. **A)** While phone features are mentioned, the book is about the types of phones listed in the index.

12. **C)** Italics are used to highlight the titles of the books and to emphasize the word *twisted*, which refers to altering a story, not to something being misshapen.

13. **D)** Encyclopedias, articles, and biographies are secondary sources that provide information about a historical figure or event.

14. **A)** *Fortification* and *fortress* are synonyms. In the seventeenth century, the purpose of the fortress changed. This is a clue that *converted* means "a change in form or function."

15. **A)** The root *cred* means *believe*. The words *evidence*, *reviewed*, and *approved* are context clues hinting that something needs to be believed and accepted.

16. **D)** The author compares the food trucks to "a carnival of delicious treats," using the word *like*.

17. **B)** According to the recipe directions, the saucepan must be filled with water before the other steps listed.

18. **B)** According to the passage, a baby achieves milestones in independent movement in this order. Use the ages and signal words to determine the order of events.

19. **A)** The memo is intended to ensure that all employees are following the same email guidelines. It is a reminder of the existing policy, not a new policy, and includes instructions all employees must follow.

20. **A)** Jean will travel south from the police station to the library, passing the light once, then back up to the street where she will pass the light a second time to turn east to head to the hospital.

WRITING

GRAMMAR

Some questions on some civil service exams will test your understanding of the basic rules of grammar. To start, it is helpful to review the parts of speech and the rules that accompany them. The good news is that you have been using these rules since you first began to speak. Even if you do not know a lot of the technical terms, many of these rules will be familiar to you. Some of the topics you might see include:

- matching pronouns with their antecedents
- matching verbs with their subjects
- ensuring that verbs are in the correct tense
- using correct capitalization
- distinguishing between types of sentences
- correcting sentence structure
- identifying parts of speech

Nouns and Pronouns

NOUNS are people, places, or things. The subject of a sentence is typically a noun. For example, in the sentence "The hospital was very clean," the subject, *hospital*, is a noun; it is a place. **PRONOUNS** stand in for nouns and can be used to make sentences sound less repetitive. Take the sentence, "Sam stayed home from school because Sam was not feeling well." The word *Sam* appears twice in the same sentence. Instead, you can use the pronoun *he* to stand in for *Sam* and say, "Sam stayed home from school because he was not feeling well."

Because pronouns take the place of nouns, they need to agree both in number and gender with the noun they replace. So, a plural noun needs a plural pronoun, and a noun referring to something feminine needs a feminine pronoun. In the first sentence in this paragraph, for example, the plural pronoun

HELPFUL HINT

Some examples of singular pronouns include:

- I, me, my, mine
- you, your, yours
- he, him, his
- she, her, hers
- it, its

Some examples of plural pronouns include:

- we, us, our, ours
- they, them, their, theirs

they replaced the plural noun *pronouns*. Questions that cover pronoun agreement are common, so it's good to get comfortable spotting pronouns.

> Wrong: If a student forgets their homework, they will not receive a grade.
>
> Correct: If a student forgets his or her homework, he or she will not receive a grade.

Student is a singular noun, but *their* and *they* are plural pronouns. So, the first sentence is incorrect. To correct it, use the singular pronoun *his* or *her* or *he* or *she*.

> Wrong: Everybody will receive their paychecks promptly.
>
> Correct: Everybody will receive his or her paycheck promptly.

Everybody is a singular noun, but *their* is a plural pronoun. So, the first sentence is incorrect. To correct it, use the singular pronoun *his* or *her*.

> Wrong: When nurses scrub in to surgery, you should wash your hands.
>
> Correct: When nurses scrub in to surgery, they should wash their hands.

The first sentence begins in third-person perspective and then switches to second-person perspective. So, this sentence is incorrect. To correct it, use a third-person pronoun in the second clause.

> Wrong: After the teacher spoke to the student, she realized her mistake.
>
> Correct: After Mr. White spoke to his student, she realized her mistake. (*She* and *her* refer to the student.)
>
> Correct: After speaking to the student, the teacher realized her own mistake. (*Her* refers to the teacher.)

The first sentence refers to a teacher and a student. But whom does *she* refer to, the teacher or the student? To eliminate the ambiguity, use specific names or state more specifically who made the mistake.

Examples

1. Which of the following lists includes all the nouns in the sentence?

   I have lived in Minnesota since August, but I still don't own a warm coat or gloves.

   A) coat, gloves

   B) I, coat, gloves

   C) Minnesota, August, coat, gloves

   D) I, Minnesota, August, warm, coat, gloves

2. In which of the following sentences do the nouns and pronouns NOT agree?

   A) After we walked inside, we took off our hats and shoes and hung them in the closet.

   B) The members of the band should leave her instruments in the rehearsal room.

   C) The janitor on duty should rinse out his or her mop before leaving for the day.

   D) When you see someone in trouble, you should always try to help them.

Verbs

A **VERB** is the action of a sentence: it describes what the subject of the sentence is or is doing. Verbs must match the subject of the sentence in person and number, and must be in the proper tense—past, present, or future.

Person describes the relationship of the speaker to the subject of the sentence: first (I, we), second (you), and third (he, she, it, they). *Number* refers to whether the subject of the sentence is singular or plural. Verbs are conjugated to match the person and number of the subject.

Table 2.1. Conjugating Verbs for Person

PERSON	SINGULAR	PLURAL
First	I jump	we jump
Second	you jump	you jump
Third	he/she/it jumps	they jump

HELPFUL HINT

Think of the subject and the verb as sharing a single *s*. If the subject ends with an *s*, the verb should not, and vice versa.

> Wrong: The cat chase the ball while the dogs runs in the yard.
>
> Correct: The cat chases the ball while the dogs run in the yard.

Cat is singular, so it takes a singular verb (which confusingly ends with an *s*); dogs is plural, so it needs a plural verb.

> Wrong: The cars that had been recalled by the manufacturer was returned within a few months.
>
> Correct: The cars that had been recalled by the manufacturer were returned within a few months.

Sometimes, the subject and verb are separated by clauses or phrases. Here, the subject *cars* is separated from the verb by the relatively long phrase "that had been recalled by the manufacturer," making it more difficult to determine how to correctly conjugate the verb.

> Correct: The doctor and nurse work in the hospital.
>
> Correct: Neither the nurse nor her boss was scheduled to take a vacation.
>
> Correct: Either the patient or her parents need to sign the release forms.

HELPFUL HINT

If the subject is separated from the verb, cross out the phrases between them to make conjugation easier.

When the subject contains two or more nouns connected by *and*, that subject becomes plural and requires a plural verb. Singular subjects joined by *or*, *either/or*, *neither/nor*, or *not only/but also* remain singular; when these words join plural and singular subjects, the verb should match the closest subject.

Finally, verbs must be conjugated for tense, which shows when the action happened. Some conjugations include helping verbs like *was*, *have*, *have been*, and *will have been*.

Table 2.2. Verb Tenses

TENSE	PAST	PRESENT	FUTURE
Simple	I <u>gave</u> her a gift yesterday.	I <u>give</u> her a gift every day.	I <u>will give</u> her a gift on her birthday.
Continuous	I <u>was giving</u> her a gift when you got here.	I <u>am giving</u> her a gift; come in!	I <u>will be giving</u> her a gift at dinner.
Perfect	I <u>had given</u> her a gift before you got there.	I <u>have given</u> her a gift already.	I <u>will have given</u> her a gift by midnight.
Perfect continuous	Her friends <u>had been giving</u> her gifts all night when I arrived.	I <u>have been giving</u> her gifts every year for nine years.	I <u>will have been giving</u> her gifts on holidays for ten years next year.

Tense must also be consistent throughout the sentence and the passage. For example, the sentence "I was baking cookies and eat some dough" sounds strange. That is because the two verbs, *was baking* and *eat*, are in different tenses. *Was baking* occurred in the past; *eat*, on the other hand, occurs in the present. To make them consistent, change *eat* to *ate*.

> Wrong: Because it will rain during the party last night, we had to move the tables inside.
>
> Correct: Because it rained during the party last night, we had to move the tables inside.

All the verb tenses in a sentence need to agree both with each other and with the other information in the sentence. In the first sentence above, the tense does not match the other information in the sentence: *last night* indicates the past (*rained*), not the future (*will rain*).

Examples

3. Which of the following sentences contains an incorrectly conjugated verb?

    A) The brother and sister runs very fast.

    B) Neither Anne nor Suzy likes the soup.

    C) The mother and father love their new baby.

    D) Either Jack or Jill will pick up the pizza.

4. Which of the following sentences contains an incorrect verb tense?

    A) After the show ended, we drove to the restaurant for dinner.

    B) Anne went to the mall before she headed home.

    C) Johnny went to the movies after he cleans the kitchen.

    D) Before the alarm sounded, smoke filled the cafeteria.

Adjectives and Adverbs

ADJECTIVES provide more information about a noun in a sentence. Take the sentence, "The boy hit the ball." If you want your readers to know more about the noun *boy*, you could use an adjective to describe him: *the little boy, the young boy, the tall boy.*

ADVERBS and adjectives are similar because they provide more information about a part of a sentence. However, adverbs do not describe nouns—that's an adjective's job. Instead, adverbs describe verbs, adjectives, and even other adverbs. For example, in the sentence "The doctor had recently hired a new employee," the adverb *recently* tells us more about how the action *hired* took place.

Adjectives, adverbs, and MODIFYING PHRASES (groups of words that together modify another word) should be placed as close as possible to the word they modify. Separating words from their modifiers can create incorrect or confusing sentences.

> Wrong: Running through the hall, the bell rang and the student knew she was late.
>
> Correct: Running through the hall, the student heard the bell ring and knew she was late.

The phrase "running through the hall" should be placed next to *student*, the noun it modifies.

The suffixes *–er* and *–est* are often used to modify adjectives when a sentence is making a comparison. The suffix *–er* is used when comparing two things, and the suffix *–est* is used when comparing more than two.

> Anne is taller than Steve, but Steve is more coordinated.
>
> Of the five brothers, Billy is the funniest, and Alex is the most intelligent.

Adjectives longer than two syllables are compared using *more* (for two things) or *most* (for three or more things).

> Wrong: Of my two friends, Clara is the smartest.
>
> Correct: Of my two friends, Clara is smarter.

More and *most* should not be used in conjunction with *–er* and *–est* endings.

> Wrong: My most warmest sweater is made of wool.
>
> Correct: My warmest sweater is made of wool.

Examples

5. Which of the following lists includes all the adjectives in the sentence?

The new chef carefully stirred the boiling soup and then lowered the heat.

   A) new, boiling

   B) new, carefully, boiling

   C) new, carefully, boiling, heat

   D) new, carefully, boiling, lowered, heat

6. Which of the following sentences contains an adjective error?

   A) The new red car was faster than the old blue car.

   B) Reggie's apartment is in the tallest building on the block.

   C) The slice of cake was tastier than the brownie.

   D) Of the four speeches, Jerry's was the most long.

Other Parts of Speech

PREPOSITIONS express the location of a noun or pronoun in relation to other words and phrases described in a sentence. For example, in the sentence "The nurse parked her car in a parking garage," the preposition *in* describes the position of the car in relation to the garage. Together, the preposition and the noun that follow it are called a PREPOSITIONAL PHRASE. In this example, the prepositional phrase is "in a parking garage."

CONJUNCTIONS connect words, phrases, and clauses. The conjunctions summarized in the acronym FANBOYS—For, And, Nor, But, Or, Yet, So—are called COORDINATING CONJUNCTIONS and are used to join INDEPENDENT CLAUSES (clauses that can stand alone as a complete sentence). For example, in the following sentence, the conjunction *and* joins together two independent clauses:

> The nurse prepared the patient for surgery, and the doctor performed the surgery.

HELPFUL HINT

An independent (or main) clause can stand alone as its own sentence. A dependent (or subordinate) clause must be attached to an independent clause to make a complete sentence.

Other conjunctions, like *although*, *because*, and *if*, join together an independent and a DEPENDENT CLAUSE (which cannot stand on its own). Take the following sentence:

> She had to ride the subway because her car was broken.

The clause "because her car was broken" cannot stand on its own.

INTERJECTIONS, like *wow* and *hey*, express emotion and are most commonly used in conversation and casual writing.

Examples

Choose the word that best completes the sentence.

7. Her love _____ blueberry muffins kept her coming back to the bakery every week.

   A) to

   B) with

   C) of

   D) about

8. Christine left her house early on Monday morning, _____ she was still late for work.

   A) but

   B) and

   C) for

   D) or

CAPITALIZATION

Capitalization questions will ask you to spot errors in capitalization within a phrase or sentence. Below are the most important rules for capitalization.

The first word of a sentence is always capitalized.

> We will be having dinner at a new restaurant tonight.

The first letter of a proper noun is always capitalized.

> We're going to Chicago on Wednesday.

Titles are capitalized if they precede the name they modify.

> Joe Biden, the vice president, met with President Obama.

Months are capitalized, but not the names of the seasons.

> Snow fell in March even though winter was over.

The names of major holidays should be capitalized. The word *day* is only capitalized if it is part of the holiday's name.

> We always go to a parade on Memorial Day, but Christmas day we stay home.

The names of specific places should always be capitalized. General location terms are not capitalized.

> We're going to San Francisco next weekend so I can see the ocean.

Titles for relatives should be capitalized when they precede a name, but not when they stand alone.

> Fred, my uncle, will make fried chicken, and Aunt Betty is going to make spaghetti.

Example

9. Which of the following sentences contains an error in capitalization?
   A) My two brothers are going to New Orleans for Mardi Gras.
   B) On Friday we voted to elect a new class president.
   C) Janet wants to go to Mexico this Spring.
   D) Peter complimented the chef on his cooking.

HOMOPHONES AND SPELLING

HELPFUL HINT

Some common homophones include:

- bare/bear
- brake/break
- die/dye
- effect/affect
- flour/flower
- heal/heel
- insure/ensure
- morning/mourning
- peace/piece
- poor/pour
- principal/principle
- sole/soul
- stair/stare
- suite/sweet
- their/there/they're
- wear/where

Homophones

The exam will include questions that ask you to choose between **HOMOPHONES**, words that are pronounced the same but have different meanings. *Bawl* and *ball*, for example, are homophones: they sound the same, but the first means to cry, and the second is a round toy.

Spelling Rules

You may be tested on spelling, so it is good to familiarize yourself with commonly misspelled words and special spelling rules. You may be asked to find a misspelled word in a sentence or identify words that don't follow standard spelling rules.

Frequently (but not always!), *i* comes before *e* except after *c*.

> belief, thief, receive, ceiling

Be cautious of this rule, for it has exceptions: *Your foreign neighbors weighed the iciest beige glaciers!*

Double a final consonant when adding suffixes if the consonant is preceded by a single vowel.

> run → running
>
> admit → admittance

Drop the final vowel when adding a suffix.

> sue → suing
>
> observe → observance

Change the final *y* to an *i* when adding a suffix.

> lazy → laziest

> tidy → tidily

Regular nouns are made plural by adding *s*. Irregular nouns can follow many different rules for pluralization, which are summarized in Table 2.3.

Table 2.3. Irregular Plural Nouns

ENDS WITH . . .	MAKE IT PLURAL BY . . .	EXAMPLE
y	changing *y* to *i* and adding –*es*	baby → babies
f	changing *f* to *v* and adding –*es*	leaf → leaves
fe	changing *f* to *v* and adding –*s*	knife → knives
o	adding –*es*	potato → potatoes
us	changing –*us* to –*i*	nucleus → nuclei

ALWAYS THE SAME		DOESN'T FOLLOW THE RULES	
sheep	pants	man → men	goose → geese
deer	binoculars	child → children	mouse → mice
fish	scissors	person → people	ox → oxen
moose		tooth → teeth	

Commonly Misspelled Words

- accommodate
- across
- argument
- believe
- committee
- completely
- conscious
- discipline
- experience
- foreign
- government
- guarantee
- height
- immediately
- intelligence
- judgment
- knowledge
- license
- lightning
- lose
- maneuver
- misspell
- noticeable
- occasionally
- occurred
- opinion
- personnel
- piece
- possession
- receive
- separate
- successful
- technique
- tendency
- unanimous
- until
- usually
- vacuum
- whether
- which

10. Which of the following sentences contains a spelling error?

    A) It was unusually warm that winter, so we didn't need to use our fireplace.

    B) Our garden includes tomatos, squash, and carrots.

    C) The local zoo will be opening a new exhibit that includes African elephants.

    D) My sister is learning to speak a foreign language so she can travel abroad.

11. Which of the following words correctly completes the sentence?

    The nurse has three _____ to see before lunch.

    A) patents

    B) patience

    C) patients

    D) patience

SENTENCE STRUCTURE

Phrases

To understand what a phrase is, you have to know about subjects and predicates. The **SUBJECT** is what the sentence is about; the **PREDICATE** contains the verb and its modifiers.

> The nurse at the front desk will answer any questions you have.
>
> Subject: the nurse at the front desk
>
> Predicate: will answer any questions you have

A **PHRASE** is a group of words that communicates only part of an idea because it lacks either a subject or a predicate. Phrases are categorized based on the main word in the phrase. A **PREPOSITIONAL PHRASE** begins with a preposition and ends with an object of the preposition, a **VERB PHRASE** is composed of the main verb along with any helping verbs, and a **NOUN PHRASE** consists of a noun and its modifiers.

> Prepositional phrase: The dog is hiding under the porch.
>
> Verb phrase: The chef wanted to cook a different dish.
>
> Noun phrase: The big red barn rests beside the vacant chicken house.

Example

12. Identify the type of phrase underlined in the following sentence.

    The new patient was assigned to the nurse with the most experience.

A) prepositional phrase

B) noun phrase

C) verb phrase

D) verbal phrase

Clauses

CLAUSES contain both a subject and a predicate. They can be either independent or dependent. An INDEPENDENT (or main) CLAUSE can stand alone as its own sentence.

> The dog ate her homework.

Dependent (or subordinate) clauses cannot stand alone as their own sentences. They start with a subordinating conjunction, relative pronoun, or relative adjective, which will make them sound incomplete.

> Because the dog ate her homework

A sentence can be classified as simple, compound, complex, or compound-complex based on the type and number of clauses it has.

Table 2.4. Sentences

SENTENCE TYPE	NUMBER OF INDEPENDENT CLAUSES	NUMBER OF DEPENDENT CLAUSES
Simple	1	0
Compound	2 or more	0
Complex	1	1 or more
Compound-complex	2 or more	1 or more

A SIMPLE SENTENCE consists of one independent clause. Because there are no dependent clauses in a simple sentence, it can be a two-word sentence, with one word being the subject and the other word being the verb, such as "I ran."

However, a simple sentence can also contain prepositions, adjectives, and adverbs. Even though these additions can extend the length of a simple sentence, it is still considered a simple sentence as long as it does not contain any dependent clauses.

> San Francisco in the springtime is one of my favorite places to visit.

Although the sentence is lengthy, it is simple because it contains only one subject and one verb (*San Francisco* and *is*), modified by additional phrases.

COMPOUND SENTENCES have two or more independent clauses and no dependent clauses. Usually a comma and a coordinating conjunction (the FANBOYS: *For, And, Nor, But, Or, Yet,* and *So*) join the independent clauses, though semicolons can be used as well. The sentence "My computer broke, so I took it to be repaired" is compound.

HELPFUL HINT

On the test you will have to both identify and construct different kinds of sentences.

> The game was canceled, but we will still practice on Saturday.

This sentence is made up of two independent clauses joined by a conjunction (*but*), so it is compound.

COMPLEX SENTENCES have one independent clause and at least one dependent clause. In the complex sentence "If you lie down with dogs, you'll wake up with fleas," the first clause is dependent (because of the subordinating conjunction *if*), and the second is independent.

> I love listening to the radio in the car because I can sing along as loud as I want.

The sentence has one independent clause (*I love...car*) and one dependent (*because I...want*), so it is complex.

COMPOUND-COMPLEX SENTENCES have two or more independent clauses and at least one dependent clause. For example, the sentence "Even though David was a vegetarian, he went with his friends to steakhouses, but he focused on the conversation instead of the food," is compound-complex.

> I wanted to get a dog, but I have a fish because my roommate is allergic to pet dander.

This sentence has three clauses: two independent (*I wanted...dog* and *I have a fish*) and one dependent (*because my...dander*), so it is compound-complex.

QUICK REVIEW

Can you write a simple, compound, complex, and compound-complex sentence using the same independent clause?

Examples

13. Which of the following choices is a simple sentence?
    A) Elsa drove while Erica navigated.
    B) Betty ordered a fruit salad, and Sue ordered eggs.
    C) Because she was late, Jenny ran down the hall.
    D) John ate breakfast with his mother, brother, and father.

14. Which of the following sentences is a compound-complex sentence?
    A) While they were at the game, Anne cheered for the home team, but Harvey rooted for the underdogs.
    B) The rain flooded all of the driveway, some of the yard, and even part of the sidewalk across the street.
    C) After everyone finished the test, Mr. Brown passed a bowl of candy around the classroom.
    D) All the flowers in the front yard are in bloom, and the trees around the house are lush and green.

Punctuation

The basic rules for using the major punctuation marks are given in Table 2.5.

Table 2.5. How to Use Punctuation

PUNCTUATION	USED FOR	EXAMPLE
Period	ending sentences	Periods go at the end of complete sentences.
Question mark	ending questions	What's the best way to end a sentence?
Exclamation point	ending sentences that show extreme emotion	I'll never understand how to use commas!
Comma	joining two independent clauses (always with a coordinating conjunction)	Commas can be used to join clauses, but they must always be followed by a coordinating conjunction.
	setting apart introductory and nonessential words and phrases	Commas, when used properly, set apart extra information in a sentence.
	separating items in a list	My favorite punctuation marks include the colon, semicolon, and period.
Semicolon	joining together two independent clauses (never used with a conjunction)	I love exclamation points; they make sentences seem so exciting!
Colon	introducing a list, explanation, or definition	When I see a colon I know what to expect: more information.
Apostrophe	forming contractions	It's amazing how many people can't use apostrophes correctly.
	showing possession	Parentheses are my sister's favorite punctuation; she finds commas' rules confusing.
Quotation marks	indicating a direct quote	I said to her, "Tell me more about parentheses."

Examples

15. Which of the following sentences contains an error in punctuation?

    A) I love apple pie! John exclaimed with a smile.

    B) Jennifer loves Adam's new haircut.

    C) Billy went to the store; he bought bread, milk, and cheese.

    D) Alexandra hates raisins, but she loves chocolate chips.

16. Which punctuation mark correctly completes the sentence?

    Sam, why don't you come with us for dinner_

    A) .

    B) ?

    C) ;

    D) :

ANSWER KEY

1. **C)** *Minnesota* and *August* are proper nouns, and *coat* and *gloves* are common nouns. *I* is a pronoun, and *warm* is an adjective that modifies *coat*.

2. **B)** "The members of the band" is plural, so it should be replaced by the plural pronoun *their* instead of the singular *her*.

3. **A)** Choice A should read "The brother and sister run very fast." When the subject contains two or more nouns connected by *and*, the subject is plural and requires a plural verb.

4. **C)** Choice C should read "Johnny will go to the movies after he cleans the kitchen." It does not make sense to say that Johnny does something in the past (*went to the movies*) after doing something in the present (*after he cleans*).

5. **A)** *New* modifies the noun *chef*, and *boiling* modifies the noun *soup*. *Carefully* is an adverb modifying the verb *stirred*. *Lowered* is a verb, and *heat* is a noun.

6. **D)** Choice D should read, "Of the four speeches, Jerry's was the longest." The word *long* has only one syllable, so it should be modified with the suffix *–est*, not the word *most*.

7. **C)** The correct preposition is *of*.

8. **A)** In this sentence, the conjunction is joining together two contrasting ideas, so the correct answer is *but*.

9. **C)** *Spring* is the name of a season and should not be capitalized.

10. **B)** *Tomatos* should be spelled *tomatoes*.

11. **C)** *Patients* is the correct spelling and the correct homophone. *Patients* are people in a hospital and *patience* is the ability to avoid getting upset in negative situations.

12. **A)** The underlined section of the sentence is a prepositional phrase beginning with the preposition *with*.

13. **D)** Choice D contains one independent clause with one subject and one verb. Choices A and C are complex sentences because they each contain both a dependent and independent clause. Choice B contains two independent clauses joined by a conjunction and is therefore a compound sentence.

14. **A)** Choice A is a compound-complex sentence because it contains two independent clauses and one dependent clause. Despite its length, choice B is a simple sentence because it contains only one independent clause. Choice C is a complex sentence because it contains one dependent clause and one independent clause. Choice D is a compound sentence; it contains two independent clauses.

15. **A)** Choice A should use quotation marks to set off a direct quote: *"I love apple pie!" John exclaimed with a smile.*

16. **B)** The sentence is a question, so it should end with a question mark.

3

VERBAL and REASONING SKILLS

Vocabulary

Some portions of the civil service exam may ask you to provide definitions or intended meanings of words. These might appear within reading passages (see chapter 1), or in other verbal skills questions. A general vocabulary review follows.

You may have never previously encountered some of these words, but there are tricks you can use to figure out what they mean.

Context Clues

One of the most fundamental vocabulary skills is using the context in which a word is used to determine its meaning. Your ability to read sentences carefully is extremely useful when it comes to understanding new vocabulary words.

Vocabulary questions often include **SENTENCE CONTEXT CLUES** within the sentence that contains the word. There are several clues that can help you understand the context, and therefore the meaning of a word:

RESTATEMENT CLUES state the definition of the word in the sentence. The definition is often set apart from the rest of the sentence by a comma, parentheses, or a colon.

> Teachers often prefer teaching students with <u>intrinsic</u> motivation: these students have an <u>internal</u> desire to learn.

The meaning of *intrinsic* is restated as *internal.*

CONTRAST CLUES include the opposite meaning of a word. Words like *but, on the other hand,* and *however* are tip-offs that a sentence contains a contrast clue.

> Janet was <u>destitute</u> after she lost her job, but her wealthy sister helped her get back on her feet.

Destitute is contrasted with *wealthy*, so the definition of destitute is "poor."

PositIve/negatIve clues tell you whether a word has a positive or negative meaning.

> The film was <u>lauded</u> by critics as stunning, and was nominated for several awards.

The positive descriptions *stunning* and "nominated for several awards" suggest that *lauded* has a positive meaning.

Examples

Select the answer that most closely matches the definition of the underlined word as it is used in the sentence.

1. The dog was <u>dauntless</u> in the face of danger, braving the fire to save the girl trapped inside the building.

    A) difficult

    B) fearless

    C) imaginative

    D) startled

2. Beth did not spend any time preparing for the test, but Tyrone kept a <u>rigorous</u> study schedule.

    A) strict

    B) loose

    C) boring

    D) strange

Analyzing Words

Determining the meaning of a word can be more complicated than just looking in a dictionary. A word might have more than one DENOTATION, or definition. The definition the author intends can only be judged by looking at the surrounding text. For example, the word *quack* can refer to the sound a duck makes or to a person who publicly pretends to have a qualification which they do not actually possess.

A word may also have different CONNOTATIONS, which are the implied meanings and emotions a word evokes in the reader. For example, a cubicle is simply a walled desk in an office, but for many the word implies a constrictive, uninspiring workplace. Connotations can vary greatly between cultures and even between individuals.

Last, authors might make use of FIGURATIVE LANGUAGE, which is the use of a word to imply something other than the word's literal definition. This is often done by comparing two things. If you say "I felt like a butterfly when I got a new haircut," the listener knows you do not resemble an insect but instead felt beautiful and transformed.

Examples

Select the answer that most closely matches the definition of the underlined word or phrase as it is used in the sentence.

3. The nurse looked at the patient's eyes and determined from his uneven <u>pupils</u> that brain damage was possible.

   A) part of the eye

   B) young student

   C) walking pace

   D) breathing sounds

4. Aiden examined the antique lamp and worried that he had been <u>taken for a ride</u>. He had paid a lot for the vintage lamp, but it looked like it was worthless.

   A) transported

   B) forgotten

   C) deceived

   D) hindered

Word Structure

You are not expected to know every word in the English language for your test; rather, you will need to use deductive reasoning to find the best definition of the word in question. Many words can be broken down into three main parts to help determine their meaning:

> **PREFIX — ROOT — SUFFIX**

ROOTS are the building blocks of all words. Every word is either a root itself or has a root. The root is what is left when you strip away the prefixes and suffixes from a word. For example, in the word *unclear*, if you take away the prefix *un–*, you have the root *clear*.

Roots are not always recognizable words, because they often come from Latin or Greek words, such as *nat*, a Latin root meaning born. The word *native*, which means a person born in a referenced place, comes from this root; so does the word *prenatal*, meaning *before birth*. It is important to keep in mind, however, that roots do not always match the original definitions of words, and they can have several different spellings.

PREFIXES are elements added to the beginning of a word, and **SUFFIXES** are elements added to the end of the word; together they are known as **AFFIXES**. They carry assigned meanings and can be attached to a word to completely change the word's meaning or to enhance the word's original meaning.

Let's use the word *prefix* itself as an example: *fix* means to place something securely and *pre–* means before. Therefore, *prefix* means to place something before or in front of. Now let's look at a suffix: in the word *feminism*, *femin* is a root which means female. The suffix *–ism* means act, practice, or process. Thus, *feminism* is the process of establishing equal rights for women.

QUICK REVIEW

Can you figure out the definitions of the following words using their parts?

- ambidextrous
- anthropology
- diagram
- egocentric
- hemisphere
- homicide
- metamorphosis
- nonsense
- portable
- rewind
- submarine
- triangle
- unicycle

Although you cannot determine the meaning of a word from a prefix or suffix alone, you can use this knowledge to eliminate answer choices. Understanding whether the word is positive or negative can give you the partial meaning of the word.

Table 3.1. Common Roots

ROOT	DEFINITION	EXAMPLE
ast(er)	star	asteroid, astronomy
audi	hear	audience, audible
auto	self	automatic, autograph
bene	good	beneficent, benign
bio	life	biology, biorhythm
cap	take	capture
ced	yield	secede
chrono	time	chronometer, chronic
corp	body	corporeal
crac or crat	rule	autocrat
demo	people	democracy
dict	say	dictionary, dictation
duc	lead or make	ductile, produce
gen	give birth	generation, genetics
geo	earth	geography, geometry
grad	step	graduate
graph	write	graphical, autograph
ject	throw	eject
jur or jus	law	justice, jurisdiction
juven	young	juvenile
log or logue	thought	logic, logarithm
luc	light	lucidity
man	hand	manual
mand	order	remand
mis	send	transmission
mono	one	monotone
omni	all	omnivore
path	feel	sympathy
phil	love	philanthropy
phon	sound	phonograph
port	carry	export
qui	rest	quiet
scrib or script	write	scribe, transcript

ROOT	DEFINITION	EXAMPLE
sense or sent	feel	sentiment
tele	far away	telephone
terr	earth	terrace
uni	single	unicode
vac	empty	vacant
vid or vis	see	video, vision

Table 3.2. Common Prefixes

PREFIX	DEFINITION	EXAMPLE
a– (also an–)	not, without; to, toward; of, completely	atheist, anemic, aside, aback, anew, abashed
ante–	before, preceding	antecedent, anteroom
anti–	opposing, against	antibiotic, anticlimax
belli–	warlike, combative	belligerent, antebellum
com– (also co–, col–, con–, cor–)	with, jointly, completely	combat, cooperate, collide, confide, correspond
dis– (also di–)	negation, removal	disadvantage, disbar
en– (also em–)	put into or on; bring into the condition of; intensify	engulf, embrace
hypo–	under	hypoglycemic, hypodermic
in– (also il–, im–, ir–)	not, without; in, into, toward, inside	infertile, impossible, illegal, irregular, influence, include
intra–	inside, within	intravenous, intrapersonal
out–	surpassing, exceeding; external, away from	outperform, outdoor
over–	excessively, completely; upper, outer, over, above	overconfident, overcast
pre–	before	precondition, preadolescent, prelude
re–	again	reapply, remake
semi–	half, partly	semicircle, semiconscious
syn– (also sym–)	in union, acting together	synthesis, symbiotic
trans–	across, beyond	transdermal
trans–	into a different state	translate
under–	beneath, below; not enough	underarm, undersecretary, underdeveloped

Examples

Select the answer that most closely matches the definition of the underlined word as it is used in the sentence.

5. The <u>bellicose</u> dog will be sent to training school next week.
   A) misbehaved
   B) friendly
   C) scared
   D) aggressive

6. The new menu <u>rejuvenated</u> the restaurant and made it one of the most popular spots in town.
   A) established
   B) invigorated
   C) improved
   D) motivated

SYNONYMS AND ANTONYMS

Vocabulary questions may appear on civil service exams as synonyms or antonyms. When different words mean the same thing, they are SYNONYMS. On synonym questions, you will need to study a word and then choose its synonym. The key to doing well on synonym questions is to have a strong vocabulary.

When two words have opposite meanings, they are ANTONYMS. Just like with synonym questions, antonym questions are really just vocabulary questions. Again, the stronger your vocabulary, the better you will do on these questions.

You can use your knowledge of word structure if you're not sure of a word. Check the prefixes. Does the prefix on the word correspond to the meaning of any of the answer choices? If so, you have a hint that the words might have a related meaning. But that's not always so: be sure to study the roots of words as well.

Examples

7. Choose the synonym for the following word: ADVANCE.
   A) promote
   B) abduct
   C) destroy
   D) review

8. Choose the antonym for the following word: MICROSCOPIC.
   A) tiny
   B) unusual
   C) enormous
   D) hungry

ANALOGIES

Different versions of civil service exams may contain verbal or visual analogies. A strong vocabulary and careful, logical, step-by-step thinking will help you to do well on these questions.

What is an Analogy?

An **ANALOGY** presents two sets of words or objects that share a relationship. The relationship is generally set up using the following format:

_____ is to _____ as _____ is to _____

Let's start with an example that uses words instead of shapes.

BIRD is to FLOCK as WOLF is to PACK

In this analogy, the first word is an individual animal, and the second word represents a group of those animals. A group of birds is a flock, and a group of wolves is a pack.

Solving analogies requires you to determine the relationship between the first two words, and then use that relationship to fill in the missing word:

SAIL is to BOAT as FLY is to_____

Here, the missing word is *plane*: you sail on a boat and fly on a plane.

Examples

9. Dog is to bark as meow is to
    A) puppy.
    B) veterinarian.
    C) cat.
    D) turtle.

10. Ugly is to pretty as hungry is to
    A) thirsty.
    B) starving.
    C) empty.
    D) full.

VISUAL ANALOGIES AND SEQUENCES

On the some civil service exams, you will encounter nonverbal, or visual, analogies. These questions will be in this same format as verbal analogies, but they will use shapes instead of words. To answer these questions, you should look for the common relationships between the first two shapes.

Rotating Shapes

The first shape is rotated 90 degrees clockwise to give the second shape. To find the missing shape, rotate the cube 90 degrees clockwise as well.

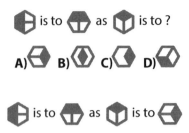

Adding to Shapes

To create the second shape, another diamond is added inside the first. To find the missing shape, add another circle inside the first one.

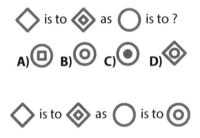

Subtracting from Shapes

The bottom diamond is removed from the first shape to create the second. To find the missing shape, remove the bottom circle.

Combinations

In this question, the first shape is reflected horizontally (as if shown in a mirror). Then, another circle is added to the end of the top line. To find the missing shape, reflect the given shape and add a circle to the end of the top line.

SEQUENCES questions use images, letters, or numeric series to test your reasoning ability. You will have to figure out the next image in a series.

Even though you might see numbers, these are not math questions. These questions are testing your ability to predict sequences and series.

Examples

11. ⬂ is to ◐ as ⬂ is to ?

A) ● B) ◐ C) ⬂ D) ◑

12. △ is to ☐ as ⬠ is to ?

A) ◺ B) ▭ C) ⬡ D) ◯

1. **B)** Demonstrating bravery in the face of danger would be *fearless*. The restatement clue (*braving*) tells you exactly what the word means.

2. **A)** The word *but* tells us that Tyrone studied in a different way than Beth, which means it is a contrast clue. If Beth did not study hard, then Tyrone did. The best answer, therefore, is choice A.

3. **A)** Only choice A matches both the definition of the word and context of the sentence. Choice B is an alternative definition for pupil, but does not make sense in the sentence. Both C and D could be correct in the context of the sentence, but neither is a definition of pupil.

4. **C)** It is clear from the context of the sentence that Aiden was not literally taken for a ride. Instead, this phrase is an example of figurative language. From context clues you can figure out that Aiden paid too much for the lamp, so he was deceived.

5. **D)** The prefix *belli–*, which means "warlike," can be used to confirm that "aggressive" is the right answer.

6. **B)** All the answer choices could make sense in the context of the sentence, so it is necessary to use word structure to find the definition. The root *juven* means young and the prefix *re–* means again, so *rejuvenate* means to be made young again. The answer choice with the most similar meaning is *invigorated*, which means to give something energy.

7. **A)** "Advance" and "promote" both mean to move something or someone forward. Note the prefix *ad–* in "advance." The prefix *ad–* means toward. Likewise, the prefix *pro–* in "promote" means forward. That's a clue that the words are related. To advance something is to promote it, to push it forward.

8. **C)** The antonym for "microscopic" is "large." First, determine the meaning of the word in question. The word "microscopic" means small or tiny. One clue is the prefix *micro–*, which means small. Choice A must be incorrect because it is a synonym for microscopic, not an antonym. Choices B and D are not related to the word in this context. Choice C, "enormous," means large. That makes it an antonym for microscopic.

9. **C)** Dogs bark; cats meow.

10. **D)** Ugly and pretty are opposites, or antonyms. Hungry and full are also opposites.

11. **D)** Rotate the first shape 90 degrees clockwise to create the second shape.

12. **C)** Add one side to the first shape to create the second shape.

4

MATHEMATICS

THE MOST COMMON MISTAKES

People make little mistakes all the time, but during a test those tiny mistakes can make the difference between a good score and a poor one. Watch out for these common mistakes that people make on the math section of the civil service exams:

- answering with the wrong sign (positive/negative)
- mixing up the order of operations
- misplacing a decimal
- not reading the question thoroughly (and therefore providing an answer that was not asked for)
- circling the wrong letter or filling in wrong circle choice

If you're thinking, *those ideas are just common sense*, that's exactly the point. Most of the mistakes made on civil service exams are simple ones. But no matter how silly the mistake, a wrong answer still means a lost point on the test.

STRATEGIES FOR THE MATHEMATICS SECTION

Go Back to the Basics

First and foremost, practice your basic skills: sign changes, order of operations, simplifying fractions, and equation manipulation. These are the skills used most on civil service exam math sections, though they are applied in different contexts. Remember that when it comes down to it, all math problems rely on the four basic skills of addition, subtraction, multiplication, and division. All you need to figure out is the order in which they're used to solve a problem.

Don't Rely on Mental Math

Using mental math is great for eliminating answer choices, but ALWAYS WRITE DOWN YOUR WORK! This cannot be stressed enough. Use whatever paper is provided; by writing and/or drawing out the problem, you are more likely to catch any mistakes. The act of writing things down also forces you to organize your calculations, leading to an improvement in your score.

The Three-Times Rule

You should read each question at least three times to ensure you're using the correct information and answering the right question:

1. Read the question and write out the given information.

2. Read the question, set up your equation(s), and solve.

3. Read the question and check that your answer makes sense (is the amount too large or small; is the answer in the correct unit of measure, etc.).

Make an Educated Guess

Eliminate those answer choices which you are relatively sure are incorrect, and then guess from the remaining choices. Educated guessing is critical to increasing your score.

NUMBERS AND OPERATIONS

Positive and Negative Number Rules

Adding, multiplying, and dividing numbers can yield positive or negative values depending on the signs of the original numbers. Knowing these rules can help determine if your answer is correct.

- (+) + (–) = the sign of the larger number
- (–) + (–) = negative number
- (–) × (–) = positive number
- (–) × (+) = negative number
- (–) ÷ (–) = positive number
- (–) ÷ (+) = negative number

Examples

1. Find the product of –10 and 47.

2. What is the sum of –65 and –32?

3. Is the product of –7 and 4 less than –7, between –7 and 4, or greater than 4?

4. What is the value of –16 divided by 2.5?

Order of Operations

Operations in a mathematical expression are always performed in a specific order, which is described by the acronym PEMDAS:

1. Parentheses
2. Exponents
3. Multiplication
4. Division
5. Addition
6. Subtraction

Perform the operations within parentheses first, and then address any exponents. After those steps, perform all multiplication and division. These are carried out from left to right as they appear in the problem.

Finally, do all required addition and subtraction, also from left to right as each operation appears in the problem.

TEST TIP

Can you come up with a mnemonic device to help yourself remember the order of operations?

Examples

5. Solve: $[-(2)^2 - (4 + 7)]$

6. Solve: $(5)^2 \div 5 + 4 \times 2$

7. Solve the expression: $15 \times (4 + 8) - 3^3$

8. Solve the expression: $\left(\frac{5}{2} \times 4\right) + 23 - 4^2$

Greatest Common Factor

The greatest common factor (GCF) of a set of numbers is the largest number that can evenly divide into all of the numbers in the set. To find the GCF of a set, find all of the factors of each number in the set. A factor is a whole number that can be multiplied by another whole number to result in the original number. For example, the number 10 has four factors: 1, 2, 5, and 10. (When listing the factors of a number, remember to include 1 and the number itself.) The largest number that is a factor for each number in the set is the GCF.

Examples

9. Find the greatest common factor of 24 and 18.

10. Find the greatest common factor of 121 and 44.

11. First aid kits are being assembled at a summer camp. A complete first aid kit requires bandages, sutures, and sterilizing swabs, and each of the kits must be identical to other kits. If the camp's total supplies include 52 bandages, 13 sutures, and 39 sterilizing swabs, how many complete first aid kits can be assembled without having any leftover materials?

12. Elena is making sundaes for her friends. She has 20 scoops of chocolate ice cream and 16 scoops of strawberry. If she wants to make identical sundaes and use all of her ice cream, how many sundaes can she make?

Comparison of Rational Numbers

HELPFUL HINT

The strategies for comparing numbers can also be used to put numbers in order from least to greatest (or vice versa).

Number comparison problems present numbers in different formats and ask which is larger or smaller, or whether the numbers are equivalent. The important step in solving these problems is to convert the numbers to the same format so that it is easier to see how they compare. If numbers are given in the same format, or after they have been converted, determine which number is smaller or if the numbers are equal. Remember that for negative numbers, higher numbers are actually smaller.

Examples

13. Is $4\frac{3}{4}$ greater than, equal to, or less than $\frac{18}{4}$?

14. Which of the following numbers has the greatest value: 104.56, 104.5, or 104.6?

15. Is 65% greater than, less than, or equal to $\frac{13}{20}$?

Units of Measurement

HELPFUL HINT

You'll be given conversion factors if they're needed for a problem, but it's still good to familiarize yourself with common ones before the test.

It can be helpful to memorize some units of measurement. These are given below. When doing unit conversion problems (i.e., when converting one unit to another), find the conversion factor, then apply that factor to the given measurement to find the new units.

Table 4.1. Unit Prefixes

PREFIX	SYMBOL	MULTIPLICATION FACTOR
tera	T	1,000,000,000,000
giga	G	1,000,000,000
mega	M	1,000,000
kilo	k	1,000
hecto	h	100
deca	da	10
base unit	--	--
deci	d	0.1
centi	c	0.01
milli	m	0.001
micro	μ	0.0000001
nano	n	0.0000000001
pico	p	0.0000000000001

Table 4.2. Units and Conversion Factors

DIMENSION	AMERICAN	SI
length	inch/foot/yard/mile	meter
mass	ounce/pound/ton	gram
volume	cup/pint/quart/gallon	liter
force	pound-force	newton
pressure	pound-force per square inch	pascal
work and energy	cal/British thermal unit	joule
temperature	Fahrenheit	kelvin
charge	faraday	coulomb

CONVERSION FACTORS

1 in. = 2.54 cm	1 lb. = 0.454 kg
1 yd. = 0.914 m	1 cal = 4.19 J
1 mi. = 1.61 km	$1°F = \frac{5}{9}(°F - 32°C)$
1 gal. = 3.785 L	1 cm³ = 1 mL
1 oz. = 28.35 g	1 hr = 3600 s

Examples

16. A fence measures 15 ft. long. How many yards long is the fence?

17. A pitcher can hold 24 cups. How many gallons can it hold?

18. A spool of wire holds 144 in. of wire. If Mario has 3 spools, how many feet of wire does he have?

19. A ball rolling across a table travels 6 inches per second. How many feet will it travel in 1 minute?

20. How many millimeters are in 0.5 m?

21. A lead ball weighs 38 g. How many kilograms does it weigh?

22. How many cubic centimeters are in 10 L?

23. Jennifer's pencil was initially 10 centimeters long. After she sharpened it, it was 9.6 centimeters long. How many millimeters did she lose from her pencil by sharpening it?

Decimals and Fractions
ADDING AND SUBTRACTING DECIMALS

When adding and subtracting decimals, line up the numbers so that the decimals are aligned. You want to subtract the ones place from the ones place, the tenths place from the tenths place, etc.

Examples

24. Find the sum of 17.07 and 2.52.

25. Jeannette has 7.4 gallons of gas in her tank. After driving, she has 6.8 gallons. How many gallons of gas did she use?

MULTIPLYING AND DIVIDING DECIMALS

When multiplying decimals, start by multiplying the numbers normally. You can then determine the placement of the decimal point in the result by adding the number of digits after the decimal in each of the numbers you multiplied together.

When dividing decimals, you should move the decimal point in the divisor (the number you're dividing by) until it is a whole. You can then move the decimal in the dividend (the number you're dividing into) the same number of places in the same direction. Finally, divide the new numbers normally to get the correct answer.

Examples

26. What is the product of 0.25 and 1.4?

27. Find $0.8 \div 0.2$.

28. Find the quotient when 40 is divided by 0.25.

WORKING WITH FRACTIONS

FRACTIONS are made up of two parts: the NUMERATOR, which appears above the bar, and the DENOMINATOR, which is below it. If a fraction is in its SIMPLEST FORM, the numerator and the denominator share no common factors. A fraction with a numerator larger than its denominator is an IMPROPER FRACTION; when the denominator is larger, it's a PROPER FRACTION.

Improper fractions can be converted into proper fractions by dividing the numerator by the denominator. The resulting whole number is placed to the left of the fraction, and the remainder becomes the new numerator; the denominator does not change. The new number is called a MIXED NUMBER because it contains a whole number and a fraction. Mixed numbers can be turned into improper fractions through the reverse process: multiply the whole number by the denominator and add the numerator to get the new numerator.

Examples

29. Simplify the fraction $\frac{121}{77}$.

30. Convert $\frac{37}{5}$ into a proper fraction.

MULTIPLYING AND DIVIDING FRACTIONS

To multiply fractions, convert any mixed numbers into improper fractions and multiply the numerators together and the denominators together. Reduce to lowest terms if needed.

To divide fractions, first convert any mixed fractions into single fractions. Then, invert the second fraction so that the denominator and numerator are switched. Finally, multiply the numerators together and the denominators together.

HELPFUL HINT

Inverting a fraction changes multiplication to division:
$\frac{a}{b} \div \frac{c}{d} = \frac{a}{b} \times \frac{d}{c} = \frac{ad}{bc}$

Examples

31. What is the product of $\frac{1}{12}$ and $\frac{6}{8}$?

32. Find $\frac{7}{8} \div \frac{1}{4}$.

33. What is the quotient of $\frac{2}{5} \div 1\frac{1}{5}$?

34. A recipe calls for $\frac{1}{4}$ cup of sugar. If 8.5 batches of the recipe are needed, how many cups of sugar will be used?

HELPFUL HINT

The quotient is the result you get when you divide two numbers.

ADDING AND SUBTRACTING FRACTIONS

Adding and subtracting fractions requires a COMMON DENOMINATOR. To find the common denominator, you can multiply each fraction by the number 1. With fractions, any number over itself (e.g., $\frac{5}{5}$, $\frac{12}{12}$, etc.) is equivalent to 1, so multiplying by such a fraction can change the denominator without changing the value of the fraction. Once the denominators are the same, the numerators can be added or subtracted.

To add mixed numbers, you can first add the whole numbers and then the fractions. To subtract mixed numbers, convert each number to an improper fraction, then subtract the numerators.

Examples

35. Simplify the expression $\frac{2}{3} - \frac{1}{5}$.

36. Find $2\frac{1}{3} - \frac{3}{2}$.

37. Find the sum of $\frac{9}{16}$, $\frac{1}{2}$, and $\frac{7}{4}$.

38. Sabrina has $\frac{2}{3}$ of a can of red paint. Her friend Amos has $\frac{1}{6}$ of a can. How much red paint do they have combined?

HELPFUL HINT

The phrase *simplify the expression* just means you need to perform all the operations in the expression.

CONVERTING FRACTIONS TO DECIMALS

Some test takers find it intimidating to handle fractions and decimals. However, there are several techniques you can use to help you convert between the two forms.

The first thing to do is simply memorize common decimals and their fractional equivalents; a list of these is given in Table 4.3. With these values, it's possible to convert more complicated fractions as well. For example, $\frac{2}{5}$ is just $\frac{1}{5}$ multiplied by 2, so $\frac{2}{5} = 0.2 \times 2 = 0.4$.

Table 4.3. Common Decimals and Fractions

FRACTION	DECIMAL
$\frac{1}{2}$	0.5
$\frac{1}{3}$	$0.\overline{33}$
$\frac{1}{4}$	0.25
$\frac{1}{5}$	0.2
$\frac{1}{6}$	$0.1\overline{66}$
$\frac{1}{7}$	$0.\overline{142857}$
$\frac{1}{8}$	0.125
$\frac{1}{9}$	$0.\overline{11}$
$\frac{1}{10}$	0.1

Knowledge of common decimal equivalents to fractions can also help you estimate. This skill can be particularly helpful on multiple-choice tests like the civil service exams, where excluding incorrect answers can be just as helpful as knowing how to find the right one. For example, to find $\frac{5}{8}$ in decimal form for an answer, you can eliminate any answers less than 0.5 because $\frac{4}{8} = 0.5$. You may also know that $\frac{6}{8}$ is the same as $\frac{3}{4}$ or 0.75, so anything above 0.75 can be eliminated as well.

Another helpful trick can be used if the denominator is easily divisible by 100: in the fraction $\frac{9}{20}$, you know 20 goes into 100 five times, so you can multiply the top and bottom by 5 to get $\frac{45}{100}$ or 0.45.

If none of these techniques work, you'll need to find the decimal by dividing the denominator by the numerator using long division.

Examples

39. Write $\frac{8}{18}$ as a decimal.

40. Write the fraction $\frac{3}{16}$ as a decimal.

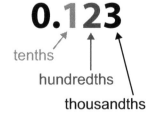

Figure 4.1. Simplified Decimal

CONVERTING DECIMALS TO FRACTIONS

Converting a decimal into a fraction is more straightforward than the reverse process is. To convert a decimal, simply use the numbers that come after the decimal as the numerator in the fraction. The denominator will be a power of 10 that matches the place value for the original decimal. For example, the denominator for 0.46 would be 100 because the last number is in the hundreths place; likewise, the denominator for 0.657 would be 1000 because the last number is in the thousandths place. Once this fraction has been set up, all that's left is to simplify it.

Example

41. Convert 0.45 into a fraction.

Ratios

A **RATIO** tells you how many of one thing exists in relation to the number of another thing. Unlike fractions, ratios do not give a part relative to a whole; instead, they compare two values. For example, if you have 3 apples and 4 oranges, the ratio of apples to oranges is 3 to 4. Ratios can be written using words (3 to 4), fractions $\left(\frac{3}{4}\right)$, or colons (3:4).

In order to work with ratios, it's helpful to rewrite them as a fraction expressing a part to a whole. For example, in the example above you have 7 total pieces of fruit, so the fraction of your fruit that are apples is $\frac{3}{7}$, and oranges make up $\frac{4}{7}$ of your fruit collection.

One last important thing to consider when working with ratios is the units of the values being compared. On some civil service mathematics exams, you may be asked to rewrite a ratio using the same units on both sides. For example, you might have to rewrite the ratio 3 minutes to 7 seconds as 180 seconds to 7 seconds.

Examples

42. There are 90 voters in a room, and each is either a Democrat or a Republican. The ratio of Democrats to Republicans is 5:4. How many Republicans are there?

43. The ratio of students to teachers in a school is 15:1. If there are 38 teachers, how many students attend the school?

Proportions

A **PROPORTION** is an equation which states that 2 ratios are equal. Proportions are usually written as 2 fractions joined by an equal sign $\left(\frac{a}{b} = \frac{c}{d}\right)$, but they can also be written using colons ($a : b :: c : d$). Note that in a proportion, the units must be the same in both numerators and in both denominators.

Often you will be given 3 of the values in a proportion and asked to find the 4th. In these types of problems, you can solve for the missing variable by cross-multiplying—multiply the numerator of each fraction by the denominator of the other to get an equation with no fractions as shown below. You can then solve the equation using basic algebra. (For more on solving basic equations, see *Algebraic Expressions and Equations*.)

$$\frac{a}{b} = \frac{c}{d} \rightarrow ad = bc$$

HELPFUL HINT
You'll see ratios written using fractions and colons on the test.

Examples

44. A train traveling 120 miles takes 3 hours to get to its destination. How long will it take for the train to travel 180 miles?

45. One acre of wheat requires 500 gallons of water. How many acres can be watered with 2600 gallons?

46. If $35 : 5 :: 49 : x$, find x.

Percentages

A **PERCENT** is the ratio of a part to the whole. Questions may give the part and the whole and ask for the percent, or give the percent and the whole and ask for the part, or give the part and the percent and ask for the value of the whole. The equation for percentages can be rearranged to solve for any of these:

$$\text{percent} = \frac{\text{part}}{\text{whole}} \qquad \text{part} = \text{whole} \times \text{percent} \qquad \text{whole} = \frac{\text{part}}{\text{percent}}$$

In the equations above, the percent should always be expressed as a decimal. In order to convert a decimal into a percentage value, simply multiply it by 100. So, if you've read 5 pages (the part) of a 10-page article (the whole), you've read $\frac{5}{10} = 0.5$ or 50%. (The percent sign (%) is used once the decimal has been multiplied by 100.)

Note that when solving these problems, the units for the part and the whole should be the same. If you're reading a book, saying you've read 5 pages out of 15 chapters doesn't make any sense.

HELPFUL HINT

The word *of* usually indicates what the whole is in a problem. For example, the problem might say *Ella ate two slices of the pizza*, which means the pizza is the whole.

Examples

47. 45 is 15% of what number?

48. Jim spent 30% of his paycheck at the fair. He spent $15 for a hat, $30 for a shirt, and $20 playing games. How much was his check? (Round to nearest dollar.)

49. What percent of 65 is 39?

50. Greta and Max sell cable subscriptions. In a given month, Greta sells 45 subscriptions and Max sells 51. If 240 total subscriptions were sold in that month, what percent were not sold by Greta or Max?

51. Grant needs to score 75% on an exam. If the exam has 45 questions, at least how many does he need to answer correctly?

Percent Change

PERCENT CHANGE problems will ask you to calculate how much a given quantity changed. The problems are solved in a similar way to regular percent problems, except that instead of using the *part* you'll use the *amount of change*. Note that the sign of the *amount of change* is important: if the original amount has increased the change will be positive, and if it has decreased the change will be

HELPFUL HINT

Words that indicate a percent change problem: *discount, markup, sale, increase,* and *decrease.*

negative. Again, in the equations below the percent is a decimal value; you need to multiply by 100 to get the actual percentage.

$$\text{percent change} = \frac{\text{amount of change}}{\text{original amount}}$$

$$\text{amount of change} = \text{original amount} \times \text{percent change}$$

$$\text{original amount} = \frac{\text{amount of change}}{\text{percentage change}}$$

Examples

52. A computer software retailer marks up its games by 40% above the wholesale price when it sells them to customers. Find the price of a game for a customer if the game costs the retailer $25.

53. A golf shop pays its wholesaler $40 for a certain club, and then sells it to a golfer for $75. What is the markup rate?

54. A store charges a 40% markup on the shoes it sells. How much did the store pay for a pair of shoes purchased by a customer for $63?

55. An item originally priced at $55 is marked 25% off. What is the sale price?

56. James wants to put in an 18 foot by 51 foot garden in his backyard. If he does, it will reduce the size of this yard by 24%. What will be the area of the remaining yard?

Probabilities

A **PROBABILITY** is found by dividing the number of desired outcomes by the number of total possible outcomes. As with percentages, a probability is the ratio of a part to a whole, with the whole being the total number of things that could happen, and the part being the number of those things that would be considered a success. Probabilities can be written using percentages (40%), decimals (0.4), fractions $\left(\frac{2}{5}\right)$, or in words (probability is 2 in 5).

$$\text{probability} = \frac{\text{desired outcomes}}{\text{total possible outcomes}}$$

Examples

57. A bag holds 3 blue marbles, 5 green marbles, and 7 red marbles. If you pick one marble from the bag, what is the probability it will be blue?

58. A bag contains 75 balls. If the probability that a ball selected from the bag will be red is 0.6, how many red balls are in the bag?

59. A theater has 230 seats: 75 seats are in the orchestra area, 100 seats are in the mezzanine, and 55 seats are in the balcony. If a ticket is selected at random, what is the probability that it will be for either a mezzanine or balcony seat?

60. The probability of selecting a student whose name begins with the letter *s* from a school attendance log is 7%. If there are 42 students whose names begin with *s* enrolled at the school, how many students attend the school?

ALGEBRA

Most civil service mathematics exams do not feature algebra. Still, it is helpful to review the basics in the event you encounter algebraic expressions.

Algebraic Expressions and Equations

Algebraic expressions and equations include a **VARIABLE**, which is a letter standing in for a number. These expressions and equations are made up of **TERMS**, which are groups of numbers and variables (e.g., $2xy$). An **EXPRESSION** is simply a set of terms (e.g., $3x + 2xy$), while an **EQUATION** includes an equal sign (e.g., $3x + 2xy = 17$). When simplifying expressions or solving algebraic equations, you'll need to use many different mathematical properties and operations, including addition, subtraction, multiplication, division, exponents, roots, distribution, and the order of operations.

EVALUATING ALGEBRAIC EXPRESSIONS

To evaluate an algebraic expression, simply plug the given value(s) in for the appropriate variable(s) in the expression.

Example

61. Evaluate $2x + 6y - 3z$ if , $x = 2$, $y = 4$, and $z = -3$.

ADDING AND SUBTRACTING TERMS

Only **LIKE TERMS**, which have the exact same variable(s), can be added or subtracted. **CONSTANTS** are numbers without variables attached, and those can be added and subtracted together as well. When simplifying an expression, like terms should be added or subtracted so that no individual group of variables occurs in more than one term. For example, the expression $5x + 6xy$ is in its simplest form, while $5x + 6xy - 11xy$ is not because the term xy appears more than once.

Example

62. Simplify the expression $5xy + 7y + 2yz + 11xy - 5yz$.

MULTIPLYING AND DIVIDING TERMS

To multiply a single term by another, simply multiply the coefficients and then multiply the variables. Remember that when multiplying variables with exponents, those exponents are added together. For example, $(x^5y)(x^3y^4) = x^8y^5$.

When multiplying a term by a set of terms inside parentheses, you need to **DISTRIBUTE** to each term inside the parentheses as shown in Figure 4.2.

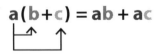

Figure 4.2. Distribution

When variables occur in both the numerator and denominator of a fraction, they cancel each other out. So, a fraction with variables in its simplest form will not have the same variable on the top and bottom.

Examples

63. Simplify the expression: $(3x^4y^2z)(2y^4z^5)$.

64. Simplify the expression: $(2y^2)(y^3 + 2xy^2z + 4z)$.

65. Simplify the expression: $(5x + 2)(3x + 3)$.

66. Simplify the expression: $\frac{2x^4y^3z}{8x^2z^2}$

SOLVING EQUATIONS

To solve an equation, you need to manipulate the terms on each side to isolate the variable, meaning if you want to find x, you have to get the x alone on one side of the equal sign. To do this, you'll need to use many of the tools discussed above: you might need to distribute, divide, add, or subtract like terms, or find common denominators.

Think of each side of the equation as the two sides of a see-saw. As long as the two people on each end weigh the same amount the see-saw will be balanced: if you have a 120 lb. person on each end, the see-saw is balanced. Giving each of them a 10 lb. rock to hold changes the weight on each end, but the see-saw itself stays balanced. Equations work the same way: you can add, subtract, multiply, or divide whatever you want as long as you do the same thing to both sides.

Equations are rare on civil service exams, but if you see them, you can solve them using the same basic steps:

1. Distribute to get rid of parentheses.
2. Use the least common denominator to get rid of fractions.
3. Add/subtract like terms on either side.
4. Add/subtract so that constants appear on only one side of the equation.
5. Multiply/divide to isolate the variable.

Examples

67. Solve for x: $25x + 12 = 62$

68. Solve the following equation for x: $2x - 4(2x + 3) = 24$

69. Solve the following equation for x: $\frac{x}{3} + \frac{1}{2} = \frac{x}{6} - \frac{5}{12}$

70. Find the value of x: $2(x + y) - 7x = 14x + 3$

Solving Word Problems

Any of the math concepts discussed here can be turned into a word problem, and you'll likely see word problems in various forms throughout the test. (In fact, you may have noticed that several examples in the ratio and proportion sections were word problems.)

The most important step in solving any word problem is to read the entire problem before beginning to solve it: one of the most commonly made mistakes on word problems is providing an answer to a question that wasn't asked. Also, remember that not all of the information given in a problem is always needed to solve it.

When working multiple-choice word problems, it's important to check your answer. Many of the incorrect choices will be answers that test takers arrive at by making common mistakes. So even if an answer you calculated is given as an answer choice, that doesn't necessarily mean you've worked the problem correctly—you have to check your own work to make sure.

GENERAL STEPS FOR WORD PROBLEM SOLVING

STEP 1: Read the entire problem and determine what the question is asking for.

STEP 2: List all of the given data and define the variables.

STEP 3: Determine the formula(s) needed or set up equations from the information in the problem.

STEP 4: Solve.

STEP 5: Check your answer. (Is the amount too large or small? Are the answers in the correct unit of measure?)

KEY WORDS

Word problems generally contain key words that can help you determine what math processes may be required in order to solve them.

- Addition: added, combined, increased by, in all, total, perimeter, sum, and more than
- Subtraction: how much more, less than, fewer than, exceeds, difference, and decreased
- Multiplication: of, times, area, and product
- Division: distribute, share, average, per, out of, percent, and quotient
- Equals: is, was, are, amounts to, and were

BASIC WORD PROBLEMS

A word problem in algebra is just an equation or a set of equations described using words. Your task when solving these problems is to turn the "story" of the problem into mathematical equations.

Examples

71. A store owner bought a case of 48 backpacks for $476.00. He sold 17 of the backpacks in his store for $18 each, and the rest were sold to a school for $15 each. What was the salesman's profit?

72. Thirty students in Mr. Joyce's room are working on projects over 2 days. The first day, he gave them $\frac{3}{5}$ of an hour to work. On the second day, he gave them half as much time as the first day. How much time did each student have to work on the project?

HELPFUL HINT
Converting units can often help you avoid operations with fractions when dealing with time.

DISTANCE WORD PROBLEMS

Distance word problems involve something traveling at a constant or average speed. Whenever you read a problem that involves *how fast*, *how far*, or *for how long*, you should think of the distance equation, $d = rt$, where d stands for distance, r for rate (speed), and t for time.

These problems can be solved by setting up a grid with d, r, and t along the top and each moving object on the left. When setting up the grid, make sure the units are consistent. For example, if the distance is in meters and the time is in seconds, the rate should be meters per second.

Examples

73. Will drove from his home to the airport at an average speed of 30 mph. He then boarded a helicopter and flew to the hospital with an average speed of 60 mph. The entire distance was 150 miles, and the trip took 3 hours. Find the distance from the airport to the hospital.

74. Two cyclists start at the same time from opposite ends of a course that is 45 miles long. One cyclist is riding at 14 mph and the second cyclist is riding at 16 mph. How long after they begin will they meet?

WORK PROBLEMS

WORK PROBLEMS involve situations where several people or machines are doing work at different rates. Your task is usually to figure out how long it will take these people or machines to complete a task while working together. The trick to doing work problems is to figure out how much of the project each person or machine completes in the same unit of time. For example, you might calculate how much of a wall a person can paint in 1 hour, or how many boxes an assembly line can pack in 1 minute.

Once you know that, you can set up an equation to solve for the total time. This equation usually has a form similar to the equation for distance, but here *work = rate × time*.

Examples

75. Bridget can clean an entire house in 12 hours while her brother Tom takes 8 hours. How long would it take for Bridget and Tom to clean 2 houses together?

76. Farmer Dan needs to water his cornfield. One hose can water a field 1.25 times faster than a second hose. When both hoses are opened, they water the field in 5 hours. How long would it take to water the field if only the second hose is used?

77. Alex takes 2 hours to shine 500 silver spoons, and Julian takes 3 hours to shine 450 silver spoons. How long will they take, working together, to shine 1000 silver spoons?

STATISTICS AND GEOMETRY

Graphs and Charts

These questions require you to interpret information from graphs and charts; they will be pretty straightforward as long as you pay careful attention to detail. There are several different graph and chart types that may appear on some civil service mathematics exams.

BAR GRAPHS

BAR GRAPHS present the numbers of an item that exist in different categories. The categories are shown on the *x*-axis, and the number of items is shown on the *y*-axis. Bar graphs are usually used to easily compare amounts.

Examples

78. The graph below shows rainfall in inches per month. Which month had the least amount of rainfall? Which had the most?

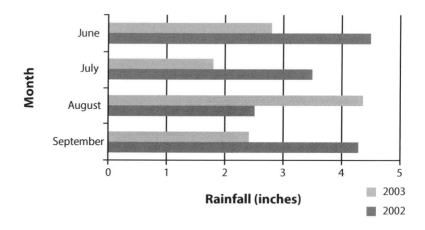

79. Using the graph below, how many more ice cream cones were sold in July than in September?

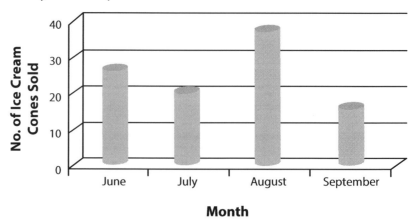

PIE CHARTS

PIE CHARTS present parts of a whole, and are often used with percentages. Together, all the slices of the pie add up to the total number of items, or 100%.

Examples

Questions 80 and 81 refer to the following pie chart showing the distribution of birthdays in a class of students.

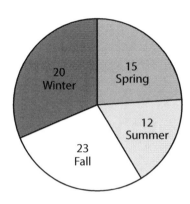

80. How many students have birthdays in the spring or summer?

81. What percentage of students have birthdays in winter?

LINE GRAPHS

LINE GRAPHS show trends over time. The number of each item represented by the graph will be on the *y*-axis, and time will be on the *x*-axis.

Examples

Questions 82 and 83 refer to the following line graph showing beverage sales at an airport snack shop throughout the day.

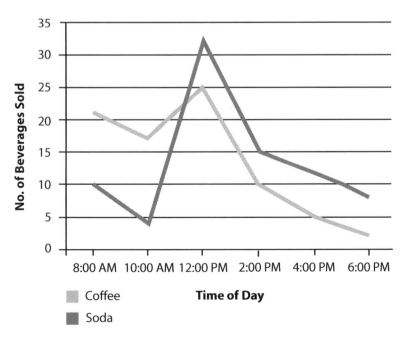

82. The line graph shows beverage sales at an airport snack shop throughout the day. Which beverage sold more at 4:00 p.m.?

83. At what time of day were the most beverages sold?

MEAN, MEDIAN, AND MODE

MEAN is a math term for average. To find the mean, total all the terms and divide by the number of terms. The **MEDIAN** is the middle number of a given set. To find the median, put the terms in numerical order; the middle number will be the median. In the case of a set of even numbers, the middle two numbers are averaged. **MODE** is the number which occurs most frequently within a given set.

HELPFUL HINT

It is possible to have more than one mode.

Examples

84. Find the mean of 24, 27, and 18.

85. The mean of three numbers is 45. If two of the numbers are 38 and 43, what is the third number?

86. What is the median of 24, 27, and 18?

87. What is the median of 24, 27, 18, and 19?

88. What is the mode of 2, 5, 4, 4, 3, 2, 8, 9, 2, 7, 2, and 2?

1. $(-) \times (+) = (-)$
   $-10 \times 47 = \mathbf{-470}$

2. $(-) + (-) = (-)$
   $-65 + -32 = \mathbf{-97}$

3. $(-) \times (+) = (-)$
   $-7 \times 4 = -28$, which is **less than −7**

4. $(-) \div (+) = (-)$
   $-16 \div 2.5 = \mathbf{-6.4}$

5. First, complete operations within parentheses:
   $(2)^2 - (11)$
   Second, calculate the value of exponential numbers:
   $-(4) - (11)$
   Finally, do addition and subtraction:
   $-4 - 11 = \mathbf{-15}$

6. First, calculate the value of exponential numbers:
   $(25) \div 5 + 4 \times 2$
   Second, calculate division and multiplication from left to right:
   $5 + 8$
   Finally, do addition and subtraction:
   $5 + 8 = \mathbf{13}$

7. First, complete operations within parentheses:
   $15 \times (12) - 3^3$
   Second, calculate the value of exponential numbers:
   $15 \times (12) - 27$
   Third, calculate division and multiplication from left to right:
   $180 - 27$
   Finally, do addition and subtraction from left to right:
   $180 - 27 = \mathbf{153}$

8. First, complete operations within parentheses:
   $(10) + 23 - 4^2$
   Second, calculate the value of exponential numbers:
   $(10) + 23 - 16$
   Finally, do addition and subtraction from left to right:
   $33 - 16 = \mathbf{17}$

9. Factors of 24: 1, 2, 3, 4, 6, 8, 12, 24

   Factors of 18: 1, 2, 3, 6, 9, 18

   The greatest common factor is 6.

10. Since these numbers are larger, it's easier to start with the smaller number when listing factors.

    Factors of 44: 1, 2, 4, 11, 22, 44

    Now, it's not necessary to list all of the factors of 121. Instead, we can eliminate those factors of 44 which do not divide evenly into 121:

    121 is not evenly divisible by 2, 4, 22, or 44 because it is an odd number. This leaves only 1 and 11 as common factors, so the **GCF is 11**.

11. This problem is asking for the greatest common factor of 52, 13, and 39. The first step is to find all of the factors of the smallest number, 13.

    Factors of 13: 1, 13

    13 is a prime number, meaning that its only factors are 1 and itself. Next, we check to see if 13 is also a factor of 39 and 52:

    $13 \times 2 = 26$

    $13 \times 3 = 39$

    $13 \times 4 = 52$

    We can see that 39 and 52 are both multiples of 13. This means that **13 first aid kits can be made without having any leftover materials.**

12. Arranging things into identical groups with no leftovers is always a tip that the problem calls for finding the greatest common factor. To find the GCF of 16 and 20, the first step is to factor both numbers:

    Factors of 16: 1, 2, 4, 8, 16

    Factors of 20: 1, 2, 4, 5, 10, 20

    From these lists, we see that **4 is the GCF**. Elena can make 4 sundaes, each with 5 scoops of chocolate ice cream and 4 scoops of strawberry. Any other combination would result in leftover ice cream or sundaes that are not identical.

13. These numbers are in different formats—one is a mixed fraction and the other is just a fraction. So, the first step is to convert the mixed fraction to a fraction:

    $$4\frac{3}{4} = 4 \times \frac{4}{4} + \frac{3}{4} = \frac{19}{4}$$

    Once the mixed number is converted, it is easier to see that $\frac{19}{4}$ **is greater than** $\frac{18}{4}$.

14. These numbers are already in the same format, so the decimal values just need to be compared. Remember that zeros can be added after the decimal without changing the value, so the three numbers can be rewritten as:

    104.56

    104.50

    104.60

    From this list, it is clearer to see that **104.60 is the greatest** because 0.60 is larger than 0.50 and 0.56.

15. The first step is to convert the numbers into the same format. 65% is the same as $\frac{65}{100}$.

Next, the fractions need to be converted to have the same denominator. It is difficult to compare fractions with different denominators. Using a factor of $\frac{5}{5}$ on the second fraction will give common denominators:

$\frac{13}{20} \times \frac{5}{5} = \frac{65}{100}$.

Now, it is easy to see that **the numbers are equivalent**.

16. 1 yd. = 3 ft.

$\frac{15}{3}$ = **5 yd.**

17. 1 gal. = 16 cups

$\frac{24}{16}$ = **1.5 gallons**

18. 12 in. = 1 ft.

$\frac{144}{12}$ = 12 ft.

12 ft. × 3 spools = **36 ft. of wire**

19. This problem can be worked in two steps: finding how many inches are covered in 1 minute, and then converting that value to feet. It can also be worked the opposite way, by finding how many feet it travels in 1 second and then converting that to feet traveled per minute. The first method is shown below.

1 min. = 60 sec.

$\frac{6 \text{ in.}}{\text{sec.}} \times 60 \text{ s} = 360$ in.

1 ft. = 12 in.

$\frac{360 \text{ in.}}{12 \text{ in.}}$ = **30 ft.**

20. 1 meter = 1000 mm

0.5 meters = **500 mm**

21. 1 kg = 1000 g

$\frac{38}{1000}$ g = **0.038 kg** .

22. 1 L = 1000 ml

10 L = 1000 ml × 10

10 L = **10,000 ml or cm³**

23. 1 cm = 10 mm

10 cm − 9.6 cm = 0.4 cm lost

0.4 cm = 10 × .4 mm = **4 mm were lost**

24.   17.07
   +   2.52
   = **19.59**

25.

$$7.4$$
$$\underline{-\ 6.8}$$
$$=\textbf{0.6 gal.}$$

26. $25 \times 14 = 350$

There are 2 digits after the decimal in 0.25 and one digit after the decimal in 1.4. Therefore the product should have 3 digits after the decimal: **0.350** is the correct answer.

27. Change 0.2 to 2 by moving the decimal one space to the right.

Next, move the decimal one space to the right on the dividend. 0.8 becomes 8.

Now, divide 8 by 2. $8 \div 2 = \textbf{4}$

28. First, change the divisor to a whole number: 0.25 becomes 25.

Next, change the dividend to match the divisor by moving the decimal two spaces to the right, so 40 becomes 4000.

Now divide: $4000 \div 25 = \textbf{160}$

29. 121 and 77 share a common factor of 11. So, if we divide each by 11 we can simplify the fraction:

$$\frac{121}{77} = \frac{11}{11} \times \frac{11}{7} = \frac{\textbf{11}}{\textbf{7}}$$

30. Convert $\frac{37}{5}$ into a proper fraction.

Start by dividing the numerator by the denominator:

$37 \div 5 = 7$ with a remainder of 2

Now build a mixed number with the whole number and the new numerator:

$$\frac{37}{5} = \textbf{7}\frac{\textbf{2}}{\textbf{5}}$$

31. Simply multiply the numerators together and the denominators together, then reduce:

$$\frac{1}{12} \times \frac{6}{8} = \frac{6}{96} = \frac{\textbf{1}}{\textbf{16}}$$

Sometimes it's easier to reduce fractions before multiplying if you can:

$$\frac{1}{12} \times \frac{6}{8} = \frac{1}{12} \times \frac{3}{4} = \frac{3}{48} = \frac{\textbf{1}}{\textbf{16}}$$

32. For a fraction division problem, invert the second fraction and then multiply and reduce:

$$\frac{7}{8} \div \frac{1}{4} = \frac{7}{8} \times \frac{4}{1} = \frac{28}{8} = \frac{\textbf{7}}{\textbf{2}}$$

33. This is a fraction division problem, so the first step is to convert the mixed number to an improper fraction:

$$1\frac{1}{5} = \frac{5 \times 1}{5} + \frac{1}{5} = \frac{6}{5}$$

Now, divide the fractions. Remember to invert the second fraction, and then multiply normally:

$$\frac{2}{5} \div \frac{6}{5} = \frac{2}{5} \times \frac{5}{6} = \frac{10}{30} = \frac{\textbf{1}}{\textbf{3}}$$

34. First, we need to convert the mixed number into a proper fraction:

$$8\frac{1}{2} = \frac{8 \times 2}{2} + \frac{1}{2} = \frac{17}{2}$$

Now, multiply the fractions across the numerators and denominators:

$$\frac{1}{4} \times \frac{17}{2} = \frac{17}{8} \textbf{ cups of sugar}$$

35. $\frac{2}{3} - \frac{1}{5}$

First, multiply each fraction by a factor of 1 to get a common denominator. How do you know which factor of 1 to use? Look at the other fraction and use the number found in that denominator:

$$\frac{2}{3} - \frac{1}{5} = \frac{2}{3}\left(\frac{5}{5}\right) - \frac{1}{5}\left(\frac{3}{3}\right) = \frac{10}{15} - \frac{3}{15}$$

Once the fractions have a common denominator, simply subtract the numerators:

$$\frac{10}{15} - \frac{3}{15} = \frac{7}{15}$$

36. $2\frac{1}{3} - \frac{3}{2}$

This is a fraction subtraction problem with a mixed number, so the first step is to convert the mixed number to an improper fraction:

$$2\frac{1}{3} = \frac{2 \times 3}{3} + \frac{1}{3} = \frac{7}{3}$$

Next, convert each fraction so they share a common denominator:

$$\frac{7}{3} \times \frac{2}{2} = \frac{14}{6}$$

$$\frac{3}{2} \times \frac{3}{3} = \frac{9}{6}$$

Now, subtract the fractions by subtracting the numerators:

$$\frac{14}{6} - \frac{9}{6} = \frac{5}{6}$$

37. $\frac{9}{16} + \frac{1}{2} + \frac{7}{4}$

For this fraction addition problem, we need to find a common denominator.

Notice that 2 and 4 are both factors of 16, so 16 can be the common denominator:

$$\frac{1}{2} \times \frac{8}{8} = \frac{8}{16}$$

$$\frac{7}{4} \times \frac{4}{4} = \frac{28}{16}$$

$$\frac{9}{16} + \frac{8}{16} + \frac{28}{16} = \frac{45}{16}$$

38. $\frac{2}{3} + \frac{1}{6}$

To add fractions, make sure that they have a common denominator. Since 3 is a factor of 6, 6 can be the common denominator:

$$\frac{2}{3} \times \frac{2}{2} = \frac{4}{6}$$

Now, add the numerators:

$$\frac{4}{6} + \frac{1}{6} = \frac{5}{6} \textbf{ of a can}$$

39. The first step here is to simplify the fraction:

$$\frac{8}{18} = \frac{4}{9}$$

Now it's clear that the fraction is a multiple of $\frac{1}{9}$, so you can easily find the decimal using a value you already know:

$$\frac{4}{9} = \frac{1}{9} \times 4 = 0.\overline{11} \times 4 = \mathbf{0.\overline{44}}$$

40. None of the tricks above will work for this fraction, so you need to do long division:

```
        0.1875
  16 | 3.0000
     −1 6
      ─────
       1 40
     − 1 28
       ─────
         120
     −   112
         ─────
          80
     −    80
          ────
           0
```

The decimal will go in front of the answer, so now you know that $\frac{3}{16} = \mathbf{0.1875}$.

41. The last number in the decimal is in the hundredths place, so we can easily set up a fraction:

$$0.45 = \frac{45}{100}$$

The next step is to simply reduce the fraction down to the lowest common denominator. Here, both 45 and 100 are divisible by 5: 45 divided by 5 is 9, and 100 divided by 5 is 20. Therefore, you're left with:

$$\frac{45}{100} = \mathbf{\frac{9}{20}}$$

42. We know that there are 5 Democrats for every 4 Republicans in the room, which means for every 9 people, 4 are Republicans.

$$5 + 4 = 9$$

Fraction of Democrats: $\frac{5}{9}$

Fraction of Republicans: $\frac{4}{9}$

If $\frac{4}{9}$ of the 90 voters are Republicans, then:

$$\frac{4}{9} \times 90 = \mathbf{40 \textbf{ voters are Republicans}}$$

43. To solve this ratio problem, we can simply multiply both sides of the ratio by the desired value to find the number of students that correspond to having 38 teachers:

$$\frac{15 \text{ students}}{1 \text{ teacher}} \times 38 \text{ teachers} = \mathbf{570 \textbf{ students}}$$

44. Start by setting up the proportion:

$$\frac{120 \text{ miles}}{3 \text{ hours}} = \frac{180 \text{ miles}}{x \text{ hours}}$$

Note that it doesn't matter which value is placed in the numerator or denominator, as long as it is the same on both sides. Now, solve for the missing quantity through cross–multiplication:

120 miles $\times$ x hours = 3 hours $\times$ 180 miles

Now solve the equation:

$$x \text{ hours} = \frac{(3 \text{ hours}) \times (180 \text{ miles})}{120 \text{ miles}}$$

$x = 4.5$ hours

45. Set up the equation:

$$\frac{1 \text{ acre}}{500 \text{ gal.}} = \frac{x \text{ acres}}{2600 \text{ gal.}}$$

Then solve for x:

$$x \text{ acres} = \frac{1 \text{ acre} \times 2600 \text{ gal.}}{500 \text{ gal.}}$$

$x = \frac{26}{5}$ or **5.2 acres**

46. This problem presents two equivalent ratios that can be set up in a fraction equation:

$$\frac{35}{5} = \frac{49}{x}$$

You can then cross-multiply to solve for x:

$35x = 49 \times 5$

$x = 7$

47. Set up the appropriate equation and solve. Don't forget to change 15% to a decimal value:

$$whole = \frac{part}{percent} = \frac{45}{0.15} = \textbf{300}$$

48. Set up the appropriate equation and solve:

$$whole = \frac{part}{percent} = \frac{15 + 30 + 20}{.30} = \textbf{\$217.00}$$

49. Set up the equation and solve:

$$percent = \frac{part}{whole} = \frac{39}{65} = \textbf{0.6 or 60\%}$$

50. You can use the information in the question to figure out what percentage of subscriptions were sold by Max and Greta:

$$percent = \frac{part}{whole} = \frac{(51 + 45)}{240} = \frac{96}{240} = 0.4 \text{ or } 40\%$$

However, the question asks how many subscriptions weren't sold by Max or Greta. If they sold 40%, then the other salespeople sold 100% − 40% = **60%**.

51. Set up the equation and solve. Remember to convert 75% to a decimal value:

part = whole $\times$ percent = $45 \times 0.75 = 33.75$, so he needs to answer at least **34 questions correctly**.

52. Set up the appropriate equation and solve:

amount of change = original amount $\times$ percent change = $25 \times 0.4 = 10$

HELPFUL HINT

The same steps shown here can be used to find percent change for problems that don't involve money as well.

If the amount of change is 10, that means the store adds a markup of $10, so the game costs:

$25 + $10 = **$35**

53. First, calculate the amount of change:

$$75 - 40 = 35$$

Now you can set up the equation and solve. (Note that *markup rate* is another way of saying *percent change*):

$$\text{percent change} = \frac{\text{amount of change}}{\text{original amount}} = \frac{35}{40} = 0.875 = \textbf{87.5\%}$$

54. You're solving for the original price, but it's going to be tricky because you don't know the amount of change; you only know the new price. To solve, you need to create an expression for the amount of change:

If original amount $= x$

Then amount of change $= 63 - x$

Now you can plug these values into your equation:

$$\text{original amount} = \frac{\text{amount of change}}{\text{percent change}}$$

$$x = \frac{63 - x}{0.4}$$

The last step is to solve for x:

$$0.4x = 63 - x$$

$$1.4x = 63$$

$$x = 45$$

The store paid **$45 for the shoes**.

55. You've been asked to find the sale price, which means you need to solve for the amount of change first:

$$\text{amount of change} = \text{original amount} \times \text{percent change}$$

$$55 \times 0.25 = 13.75$$

Using this amount, you can find the new price. Because it's on sale, we know the item will cost less than the original price:

$$55 - 13.75 = 41.25$$

The sale price is $41.25.

56. This problem is tricky because you need to figure out what each number in the problem stands for. 24% is obviously the percent change, but what about the measurements in feet? If you multiply these values you get the area of the garden:

$$18 \text{ ft.} \times 51 \text{ ft.} = 918 \text{ ft.}^2$$

This 918 ft.^{2} is the amount of change—it's how much smaller the lawn is. Now we can set up an equation:

$$\text{original amount} = \frac{\text{amount of change}}{\text{percent change}} = \frac{918}{.24} = 3825$$

If the original lawn was 3825 ft.^{2} and the garden is 918 ft.^{2}, then the remaining area is:

$$3825 - 918 = 2907$$

The remaining lawn covers **2907 ft.²**

57. Because there are 15 marbles in the bag ($3 + 5 + 7$), the total number of possible outcomes is 15. Of those outcomes, 3 would be blue marbles, which is the desired outcome. With that information you can set up an equation:

$$\text{probability} = \frac{\text{desired outcomes}}{\text{total possible outcomes}} = \frac{3}{15} = \frac{1}{5}$$

The probability is **1 in 5 or 0.2 that a blue marble is picked.**

58. Because you're solving for desired outcomes (the number of red balls), first you need to rearrange the equation:

$$\text{probability} = \frac{\text{desired outcomes}}{\text{total possible outcomes}} \rightarrow$$

$$\text{desired outcomes} = \text{probability} \times \text{total possible outcomes}$$

In this problem, the desired outcome is choosing a red ball, and the total possible outcomes are represented by the 75 total balls.

$$\text{desired outcomes} = 0.6 \times 75 = 45$$

There are **45 red balls in the bag.**

59. In this problem, the desired outcome is a seat in either the mezzanine or balcony area, and the total possible outcomes are represented by the 230 total seats, so the equation should be written as:

$$\text{probability} = \frac{\text{desired outcomes}}{\text{total possible outcomes}} = \frac{100 + 55}{230} = \mathbf{0.67}$$

60. Because you're solving for total possible outcomes (total number of students), first you need to rearrange the equation:

$$\text{total possible outcomes} = \frac{\text{desired outcomes}}{\text{probability}}$$

In this problem, you are given a probability (7% or 0.07) and the number of desired outcomes (42). These can be plugged into the equation to solve:

$$\text{total possible outcomes} = \frac{42}{0.07} = \mathbf{600\ students}$$

61. Plug in each number for the correct variable and simplify:

$$2x + 6y - 3z = 2(2) + 6(4) - 3(-3) = 4 + 24 + 9 = \mathbf{37}$$

62. Start by grouping together like terms:

$$(5xy + 11xy) + (2yz - 5yz) + 7y$$

Now you can add together each set of like terms:

$16xy + 7y - 3yz$

63. $(3x^4y^2z)(2y^4z^5)$

Multiply the coefficients and variables together:

$$3 \times 2 = 6$$
$$y^2 \times y^4 = y^6$$
$$z \times z^5 = z^6$$

Now put all the terms back together:

$6x^4y^6z^6$

64. $(2y^2)(y^3 + 2xy^2z + 4z)$

Multiply each term inside the parentheses by the term $2y^2$:

$(2y^2)(y^3 + 2xy^2z + 4z)$

$(2y^2 \times y^3) + (2y^2 \times 2xy^2z) + (2y^2 \times 4z)$

$2y^5 + 4xy^4z + 8y^2z$

65. $(5x + 2)(3x + 3)$

Use the acronym FOIL—First, Outer, Inner, Last—to multiply the terms:

First: $5x \times 3x = 15x^2$

Outer: $5x \times 3 = 15x$

Inner: $2 \times 3x = 6x$

Last: $2 \times 3 = 6$

Now combine like terms:

$15x^2 + 21x + 6$

66. $\dfrac{2x^4y^3z}{8x^2z^2}$

Simplify by looking at each variable and crossing out those that appear in the numerator and denominator:

$\dfrac{2}{8} = \dfrac{1}{4}$

$\dfrac{x^4}{x^2} = \dfrac{x^2}{1}$

$\dfrac{z}{z^2} = \dfrac{1}{z}$

$\dfrac{2x^4y^3z}{8x^2z^2} = \dfrac{x^2y^3}{4z}$

HELPFUL HINT

When multiplying terms, add the exponents. When dividing, subtract the exponents.

67. $25x + 12 = 62$

This equation has no parentheses, fractions, or like terms on the same side, so you can start by subtracting 12 from both sides of the equation:

$25x + 12 = 62$

$(25x + 12) - 12 = 62 - 12$

$25x = 50$

Now, divide by 25 to isolate the variable:

$\dfrac{25x}{25} = \dfrac{50}{25}$

$x = 2$

68. $2x - 4(2x + 3) = 24$

Start by distributing to get rid of the parentheses (don't forget to distribute the negative):

$2x - 4(2x + 3) = 24 \rightarrow 2x - 8x - 12 = 24$

There are no fractions, so now you can join like terms:

$2x - 8x - 12 = 24 \rightarrow -6x - 12 = 24$

Now add 12 to both sides and divide by −6.

$-6x - 12 = 24$

$(-6x - 12) + 12 = 24 + 12 \rightarrow -6x = 36 \rightarrow \dfrac{-6x}{-6} = \dfrac{36}{-6}$

$x = -6$

69. $\frac{x}{3} + \frac{1}{2} = \frac{x}{6} - \frac{5}{12}$

Start by multiplying by the least common denominator to get rid of the fractions:

$\frac{x}{3} + \frac{1}{2} = \frac{x}{6} - \frac{5}{12} \rightarrow 12\left(\frac{x}{3} + \frac{1}{2}\right) = 12\left(\frac{x}{6} - \frac{5}{12}\right) \rightarrow 4x + 6 = 2x - 5$

Now you can isolate x:

$(4x + 6) - 6 = (2x - 5) - 6 \rightarrow 4x = 2x - 11 \rightarrow$

$(4x) - 2x = (2x - 11) - 2x \rightarrow 2x = -11$

$\boldsymbol{x = -\frac{11}{2}}$

70. $2(x + y) - 7x = 14x + 3$

This equation looks more difficult because it has 2 variables, but you can use the same steps to solve for x. First, distribute to get rid of the parentheses and combine like terms:

$2(x + y) - 7x = 14x + 3 \rightarrow 2x + 2y - 7x = 14x + 3 \rightarrow -5x + 2y = 14x + 3$

Now you can move the x terms to one side and everything else to the other, and then divide to isolate x:

$-5x + 2y = 14x + 3 \rightarrow -19x = -2y + 3$

$\boldsymbol{x = \frac{2y - 3}{19}}$

71. Start by listing all the data and defining the variable:

total number of backpacks $= 48$

cost of backpacks $= \$476.00$

backpacks sold in store at price of $\$18 = 17$

backpacks sold to school at a price of $\$15 = 48 - 17 = 31$

total profit $= x$

Now set up an equation:

total profit = income − cost $= (306 + 465) - 476 = 295$

The store owner made a profit of **$295**.

72. Start by listing all the data and defining your variables. Note that the number of students, while given in the problem, is not needed to find the answer:

time on 1st day $= \frac{3}{5}$ hr. $= 36$ min.

time on 2nd day $= \frac{1}{2}(36) = 18$ min.

total time $= x$

Now set up the equation and solve:

total time = time on 1st day + time on 2nd day

$x = 36 + 18 = 54$

The students had **54 minutes** to work on the projects.

73. The first step is to set up a table and fill in a value for each variable:

Drive Time

	D	R	T
driving	d	30	t
flying	150 − d	60	3 − t

You can now set up equations for driving and flying. The first row gives the equation $d = 30t$, and the second row gives the equation $150 − d = 60(3 − t)$.

Next, you can solve this system of equations. Start by substituting for d in the second equation:

$d = 30t$

$150 − d = 60(3 − t) \rightarrow 150 − 30t = 60(3 − t)$

Now solve for t:

$150 − 30t = 180 − 60t$

$−30 = −30t$

$1 = t$

Although you've solved for t, you're not done yet. Notice that the problem asks for distance. So, you need to solve for d: what the problem asked for. It does not ask for time, but the time is needed to solve the problem.

Driving: $30t = 30$ miles

Flying: $150 − d = 120$ miles

The distance from the airport to the hospital is **120 miles**.

74. First, set up the table. The variable for time will be the same for each, because they will have been on the road for the same amount of time when they meet:

Cyclist Times

	D	R	T
Cyclist #1	d	14	t
Cyclist #2	45 − d	16	t

Next set up two equations:

Cyclist #1: $d = 14t$

Cyclist #2: $45 − d = 16t$

Now substitute and solve:

$d = 14t$

$45 − d = 16t \rightarrow 45 − 14t = 16t$

$45 = 30t$

$t = 1.5$

They will meet **1.5 hr.** after they begin.

75. Start by figuring out how much of a house each sibling can clean on his or her own. Bridget can clean the house in 12 hours, so she can clean $\frac{1}{12}$ of the house in an hour. Using the same logic, Tom can clean $\frac{1}{8}$ of a house in an hour.

By adding these values together, you get the fraction of the house they can clean together in an hour:

$$\frac{1}{12} + \frac{1}{8} = \frac{5}{24}$$

They can do $\frac{5}{24}$ of the job per hour.

Now set up variables and an equation to solve:

t = time spent cleaning (in hours)

h = number of houses cleaned = 2

work = rate × time

$$h = \frac{5}{24}t \rightarrow 2 = \frac{5}{24}t \rightarrow t = \frac{48}{5} = \mathbf{9\frac{3}{5} \text{ hours}}$$

76. In this problem you don't know the exact time, but you can still find the hourly rate as a variable:

The first hose completes the job in f hours, so it waters $\frac{1}{f}$ field per hour. The slower hose waters the field in 1.25f, so it waters the field in $\frac{1}{1.25f}$ hours.

Together, they take 5 hours to water the field, so they water $\frac{1}{5}$ of the field per hour.

Now you can set up the equations and solve:

$$\frac{1}{f} + \frac{1}{1.25f} = \frac{1}{5} \rightarrow$$

$$1.25f\left(\frac{1}{f} + \frac{1}{1.25f}\right) = 1.25f\left(\frac{1}{5}\right) \rightarrow 1.25 + 1 = 0.25f$$

$$2.25 = 0.25f$$

$$f = 9$$

The fast hose takes 9 hours to water the cornfield. The slower hose takes $1.25(9) = \mathbf{11.25 \text{ hours}}$.

77. Calculate how many spoons each man can shine per hour:

Alex: $\frac{500 \text{ spoons}}{2 \text{ hours}} = \frac{250 \text{ spoons}}{\text{hour}}$

Julian: $\frac{450 \text{ spoons}}{3 \text{ hours}} = \frac{150 \text{ spoons}}{\text{hour}}$

Together: $\frac{(250 + 150) \text{ spoons}}{\text{hour}} = \frac{400 \text{ spoons}}{\text{hour}}$

Now set up an equation to find the time it takes to shine 1000 spoons:

total time $= \frac{1 \text{ hour}}{400 \text{ spoons}} \times 1000 \text{ spoons} = \frac{1000}{400} \text{ hours} = \mathbf{2.5 \text{ hours}}$

78. The shortest bar represents the month with the least rain, and the longest bar represents the month with the most rain: **July 2003 had the least**, and **June 2002 had the most**.

79. Tracing from the top of each bar to the scale on the left shows that sales in July were 20 and September sales were 15. So, **5 more cones were sold in July**.

80. Fifteen students have birthdays in spring and 12 in winter, so there are **27 students** with birthdays in spring or summer.

81. Use the equation for percent:

percent $= \frac{\text{part}}{\text{whole}} = \frac{\text{winter birthdays}}{\text{total birthdays}} = \frac{20}{20 + 15 + 23 + 12} = \frac{20}{70} = \frac{2}{7} = .286$ or **28.6%**

82. At 4:00 p.m., approximately 12 sodas and 5 coffees were sold, so **more soda was sold.**

83. This question is asking for the time of day with the most sales of coffee and soda combined. It is not necessary to add up sales at each time of day to find the answer. Just from looking at the graph, you can see that sales for both beverages were highest at noon, so the answer must be **12:00 p.m.**

84. Add the terms, then divide by the number of terms:

$mean = \frac{24 + 27 + 18}{3} = \textbf{23}$

85. Set up the equation for mean with x representing the third number, then solve:

$mean = \frac{38 + 43 + x}{3} = 45$

$38 + 43 + x = 135$

$x = \textbf{54}$

86. Place the terms in order, then pick the middle term:

18, 24, 27

The median is **24.**

87. Place the terms in order. Because there are an even number of terms, the median will be the average of the middle 2 terms:

18, 19, 24, 27

$median = \frac{19 + 24}{2} = \textbf{21.5}$

88. **The mode is 2** because it appears the most within the set.

5

CLERICAL SKILLS

ALPHABETIZATION

To alphabetize words, you list them in alphabetical order (ABCDEFGHIJKLM-NOPQRSTUVWXYZ). For example, read the following list of nouns that name animals: ***jaguar***, ***elephant***, ***giraffe***, ***rhinoceros***, ***antelope***, ***chimpanzee***. In alphabetical order, this list should read as follows:

1. **a**ntelope (because *a* comes first in the alphabet)

2. **c**himpanzee (because *c* comes third in the alphabet)

3. **e**lephant (because *e* comes fifth in the alphabet; and so on)

4. **g**iraffe

5. **j**aguar

6. **r**hinoceros

Often you will be asked to alphabetize words that begin with the same letter. For example, read the following list of first names: ***Alice***, ***Andrea***, ***Alan***, ***Aaron***, ***Amber***, ***Alexander***, ***Alexandra***. To alphabetize a list like this, you will need to use the second letter in each name, the third letter in each, and so on. In alphabetical order, this list should read as follows:

1. **Aa**ron

2. **Ala**n

3. **Alexande**r

4. **Alexandr**a

5. **Ali**ce

6. **Am**ber

7. **An**drea

Aaron comes first because it begins with *Aa*. The next four names each begin with *Al* (***Alan***, ***Alexander***, ***Alexandra***, ***Alice***). In this group of four, the name ***Alan*** comes first because an *a* follows the letters *Al*. The names ***Alexander***

and *Alexandra* come after *Alan* because, in them, an *e* follows *Al*. In fact, these two names begin with the same seven letters: *Alexand*. *Alexander* comes before *Alexandra* because the man's name has an *e* following *Alexand*, while the woman's name has an *r* in the same position. The name *Alice* follows *Alexandra* because *Alice* has an *i* following *Al*, while *Alexandra* has an *e*. The last two names in the list, *Amber* and *Andrea*, begin with *Am* and *An*.

Alphabetizing Names

When alphabetizing a list of names, write the last name first, followed by a comma, followed by the first name: **Washington, George**. For example, read the following list of United States presidents' names: *Abraham Lincoln*, *Theodore Roosevelt*, *Andrew Jackson*, *John F. Kennedy*, *Barack Obama*, *Ulysses S. Grant*. In alphabetical order, this list should read as follows:

1. **G**rant, Ulysses S. (because *G* is the seventh letter in the alphabet)

2. **J**ackson, Andrew (because *J* is the tenth letter in the alphabet)

3. **K**ennedy, John F. (because *K* is the eleventh letter in the alphabet; and so on)

4. **L**incoln, Abraham

5. **O**bama, Barack

6. **R**oosevelt, Theodore

Sometimes you will need to alphabetize a list of names with the same last name. In this case, you will need to use each person's *first* name to correctly alphabetize:

1. **Roosevelt, E**leanor (because *E* is the fifth letter in the alphabet; and so on)

2. **Roosevelt, F**ranklin D.

3. **Roosevelt, T**heodore

On rare occasions, you will need to alphabetize names that have the same last name *and* the same first name. In this case, use middle initials or middle names to alphabetize. For example:

1. **Bush, George H.**W.

2. Bush, George W.

Here, the first President Bush's name comes before his son's—the second President Bush's—name because the initial *H.* comes before the initial *W.* in the alphabet.

Occasionally you may need to alphabetize a list of names like this:

1. **Watson, A.**

2. **Watson, Al**iana

3. **Watson, Aliana N.**

4. **Watson, Aliana Na**talie

Here, an initial *A.* in place of a first name precedes a spelled-out first name (*Aliana*) that begins with *A*; however, the name *Aliana Watson* with no middle initial precedes the name **Aliana N. Watson**. And the name **Aliana Natalie Watson** (with a spelled-out middle name that begins with *N*) comes last of all.

Some last names have articles and/or prepositions. Most such names originally come from languages other than English. Here are some examples:

- Names like **de la Cruz** and **De Angelo** are Spanish in origin.
- The last names **Le Boeuf** and **Du Champs** are derived from French.
- Names like **O'Donnell**, **McElmurry**, and **MacPhee** originated in Ireland or Scotland.
- Names like **van Dyke** and **van der Leyden** are Dutch.

Such last names can be spelled a variety of ways. The shorter words—the articles and prepositions—can be lower- or upper-case. There can be space or no space between the shorter and longer words. When alphabetizing last names like these, imagine each last name as all one word. Disregard apostrophes in last names such as **O'Donnell**. If you were to alphabetize a list of names with the last names shown above, the list would read as follows:

1. **De A**ngelo, Carmina
2. **de l**a Cruz, Pablo
3. **Du** Champs, Collette
4. **Le** Boeuf, John
5. **Ma**cPhee, Andrew
6. **Mc**Elmurry, Jill
7. **O'D**onnell, Jennifer
8. **van de**r Leyden, Charles
9. **van Dy**ke, Richard

Alphabetizing Business Names

When business names include people's full names, alphabetize them by last name. For example, the business names **Robyn Raymer, freelance writer** and **Jack Richardson and Sons Ltd.** should be alphabetized as follows:

1. **Ra**ymer, Robyn, freelance writer
2. **Ri**chardson, Jack, and Sons Ltd.

Business names that include numerals should be spelled out. For example, **4th Street Fish Market** should be written as **Fourth Street Fish Market**. Here is an alphabetized list of business names with numerals:

1. **For**tieth Avenue Bistro
2. **Fou**r Hundred Club, The
3. **Fourt**h Street Fish Market

When a business name includes an apostrophe or the words *the, of,* or *and,* disregard these for the purpose of alphabetizing:

1. **He**nrietta's Nest
2. **Ho**use of Hairstyling

3. Market Square, The

4. Raymond, Rex, architect

5. Raymond and **Rexf**ord, Ltd.

ALPHABETIZATION AND FILING QUESTIONS

On civil service clerical exams, you may see up to four types of alphabetization and filing questions.

Alphabetizing and Filing

The first type of question tests your general alphabetizing skills. Questions look like this:

> **DIRECTIONS:** Insert the word into the correct alphabetical position in the list. Choose the letter of the word it precedes.
>
> FELINE
>
> **A)** favored
>
> **B)** fazes
>
> **C)** felonious
>
> **D)** fighters

This type of question gives you a word and asks you where it should go in an alphabetized list. The example word, *FELINE*, belongs after the word *fazes* and before the word *felonious*. This is because the first three letters match in *feline* and *felonious*; however, the fourth letter in *feline*, *i*, precedes in alphabetical order the fourth letter in *felonious*—*o*. So, the correct answer is C: *FELINE* should be inserted before *felonious*.

Filing Names

The second type of question tests your ability to FILE NAMES. Questions look like this:

> **DIRECTIONS:** Choose the space where the given name should be filed.
>
> Brockman, Marcus L.
>
> **A)** –
>
> Bateman, Lucille R.
>
> **B)** –
>
> Brinkman, Walter Q.
>
> **C)** –
>
> Brockman, LaShawn W.
>
> **D)** –
>
> Brylls, Garner T.
>
> **E)** –

This type of question gives you a name (in this case, *Brockman, Marcus L.*) and asks you where to file it in an alphabetized list of names. Since Marcus L. Brockman shares a last name with LaShawn W. Brockman, you will need to use the first letter of each person's first name to alphabetize. Using this rule, the correct answer is D: the name *Brockman, Marcus L.* should be filed after the name *Brockman, LaShawn W.*, since *L* comes before *M* in the alphabet.

Alphabetizing Names and Businesses

The third question type tests your ability to alphabetize names and businesses. Questions look like this:

DIRECTIONS: Determine where the bolded name should be filed in the group: A if it should be first; B if it should be second; C if it should be third; D if it should be fourth.

Gary Wilson
Ronald Willis
CHIRLANE WATSON
Jeremy Wallace

A) First

B) Second

C) Third

D) Fourth

This question asks you to alphabetize a list of four names to determine in which position a boldfaced name should be placed. First, rewrite the names with the last names first: Wilson, Gary; Willis, Ronald; ***Watson, Chirlane***; and Wallace, Jeremy. Next, alphabetize the names by last name:

Wallace, Jeremy

Watson, Chirlane

Willis, Ronald

Wilson, Gary

The boldfaced name (***Watson, Chirlane***) should be filed second in the list, so the correct answer is B (Second).

Alphabetizing: Choose the Third

The fourth type of question asks you to choose the name or business that would be third in a list if the list were correctly alphabetized. Questions look like this:

DIRECTIONS: Select the name that would be *third* if the group were correctly alphabetized.

A) Isabella Washington

B) Isabella R. Washington

C) I.R. Washington

D) Isabella Rolland Washington

This question asks you to alphabetize a group of four names and then determine which name should come third in alphabetical order. First, write each name with its last name first: Washington, Isabella; Washington, Isabella R.; Washington, I.R.; Washington, Isabella Rolland. Next, alphabetize the names. According to alphabetical order, *Washington, I.R.* should precede *Washington, Isabella*:

1. Washington, I.R.
2. Washington, Isabella
3. Washington, Isabella R.
4. Washington, Isabella Rolland

Washington, Isabella R. comes third because it includes a middle initial or middle name. *Washington, I.R.* should come before *Washington, Isabella* because a first name indicated by an initial comes before a spelled-out first name that begins with the same initial. *Washington, Isabella Rolland* comes last because a middle name indicated by an initial comes before a spelled-out middle name that begins with the same initial. Thus, the correct answer is **B** (*Isabella R. Washington*); this name should come third in alphabetical order.

SPEED AND ACCURACY

Comparison Questions

There are two types of comparison questions you may encounter on civil service clerical exams. The first type looks like this:

DIRECTIONS: Read the names or numbers. Compare and decide how they relate. Mark accordingly on your answer sheet:

A) if ALL FOUR names or numbers are exactly ALIKE

B) if TWO of the names or numbers are exactly ALIKE

C) if THREE names or numbers are exactly ALIKE

D) if ALL FOUR names or numbers are DIFFERENT

1. Polly McClusky   Pollie McClusky   Polly McCluskey
   Polly McLusky

D) All four names are different.

2. 392 Spring Street   332 Spring Street   392 Spring Street
   392 Spring St.

B) Two of the addresses are exactly alike.

Here is an example of the second type of comparison question:

DIRECTIONS: Compare the sets of names and codes in each question and look for mistakes. The names and codes on the same line should be identical. Mark accordingly on your answer sheet:

A) if ALL THREE of the sets have mistakes

B) if TWO of the sets have mistakes

C) if ONE of the sets has a mistake

D) if there are NO MISTAKES in any of the sets

1. Barbara O'Rourke J7843   Barbra O'Rourke J7843
   Keira Jackson R9823   Kiera Jackson R9823
   Bradley Washington Q4557   Bradley Washington Q5457

A) All three of the sets have mistakes. In the first and second sets, the first names are spelled two different ways. The third set has different numerals in its two codes.

For comparison questions, you will be scored on both speed and accuracy. When answering practice questions, begin by focusing on accuracy. Then try to speed up as you answer comparison questions. Use whatever "speed reading" tricks work for you. Some test takers sound out abbreviations in their minds to make them sound differently from words that are spelled out. For instance, when reading this:

Spring Street   Spring St.

you might "pronounce" (silently in your mind) the abbreviation *St.* so that it sounds like *stit*. Having a strong visual memory will help you—people with this type of mind are good at spotting errors quickly. The more you practice, the stronger your visual memory will become.

Coding Questions

Some civil service clerical exams feature another type of question called coding questions. Here is an example:

DIRECTIONS: Each letter should be matched with its number as in the table below.

LETTER	NUMBER
Q	9
W	8
E	7
R	6
T	5
Y	4
U	3
P	2
S	1

Read the letters and numbers to determine if they match according to the table. Mark accordingly on your answer sheet:

A) if ALL THREE sets are correct.

B) if TWO of the sets are matched correctly.

C) if ONE of the sets is matched correctly.

D) if NONE of the sets is matched correctly.

1. PQTY   2954
      STWE   1587
      RQPU   5923

B) Two of the sets are matched correctly.

As is the case with comparison questions, the more coding questions you practice answering, the faster and more accurate you will become. Some test takers use a small cardboard rectangle to quickly focus on each letter and its matching numeral:

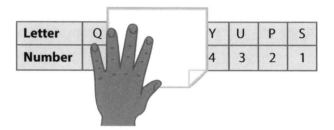

Letter	Q				Y	U	P	S
Number					4	3	2	1

Figure 5.1. Solving Coding Questions

Alternatively, you can use your index finger or a pencil to help you focus. Use whichever aid(s) work best for you. Again: the more you practice, the faster and more accurate you'll be.

Another tip for speed is to keep in mind that you may not need to read the entire code. If the first number and first letter in a set do not correspond, you already know that at least one pair in a set is incorrect. In the example above, only two of the sets are matched correctly. The incorrect set is *RQPU/5923*. The error in the set can easily be spotted by glancing at the first letter/number link. *R* should match up with *6*, not *5*. So you already know that the *RQPU/5923* set is wrong; there is no need to waste time decoding to check if the rest of the numbers correspond with the letters.

COMMUNICATION AND JUDGMENT

Civil service exams may feature **COMMUNICATION AND JUDGMENT QUESTIONS**. When answering communication and judgment questions, use your own common sense and good judgment to help you choose the correct answer to each question. Trust that the question provides all the information you will need. It is fine if you have never found yourself in the exact situation described. These are "what would *you* do if" questions meant to show your "personality" as a professional person. Here is an example:

1. An administrative assistant notices her coworker removes office supplies without accounting for them in the log. She believes the coworker is taking them home for personal use. The correct first action to take is:

A) confront the coworker and accuse him of theft and illegal personal use of government property.

B) report the coworker to the supervisor for improper use of office supplies and theft of government property.

C) ask the coworker what is happening to the missing office supplies and remind him to note them in the log.

D) ignore the situation and hope it goes away because it is none of her business.

C) The administrative assistant should start by asking her coworker about the missing supplies and reminding him to use the log. It is possible that her coworker is using the supplies honestly, and he simply forgot to note in the log the supplies he used to restock his desk or to complete work that his supervisor has asked him to do remotely. If the situation continues, then the administrative assistant should involve the supervisor.

MEMORIZATION

MEMORIZATION is the ability to recall specific evidence, facts, or details about a certain policy, event, or incident. Memorization is a key skill for civil servants. While on duty, civil servants must observe and remember the details of an event or its contexts, and they need to be alert.

On civil service examinations, memorization questions usually follow the exhibition of a particular photograph (which is viewed for a limited amount of time, usually two minutes). Candidates must recall what they witnessed in the photograph.

Review the example image below:

1. How many officers are depicted in the photograph?

A) 1

B) 2

C) 3

D) 4

2. Where was the picture most likely taken?

A) by the railroad tracks

B) at the police station

C) on the side of the road

D) in a parking lot

1. B) There are two officers in the photo.

2. C) The officers are likely standing by the side of the road. A cruiser and motorcycle are pulled over, and they are standing by brush overlooking mountains.

6

PRACTICE TEST

READING

Questions 1–6 refer to the following passage.

Hand washing is one of our simplest and most powerful weapons against infection. The idea behind hand washing is deceptively simple. Many illnesses are spread when people touch infected surfaces, such as door handles or other people's hands, and then touch their own eyes, mouths, or noses. So, if pathogens can be removed from the hands before they spread, infections can be prevented. When done correctly, hand washing can prevent the spread of many dangerous bacteria and viruses, including those that cause the flu, the common cold, diarrhea, and many acute respiratory illnesses.

The most basic method of hand washing involves only soap and water. Just twenty seconds of scrubbing with soap and a complete rinsing with water is enough to kill and/or wash away many pathogens. The process doesn't even require warm water—studies have shown that cold water is just as effective at reducing the number of microbes on the hands. Antibacterial soaps are also available, although several studies have shown that simple soap and cold water are just as effective.

In recent years, hand sanitizers have become popular as an alternative to hand washing. These gels, liquids, and foams contain a high concentration of alcohol (usually at least 60 percent) that kills most bacteria and fungi; they can also be effective against some, but not all, viruses. There is a downside to hand sanitizer, however. Because the sanitizer isn't rinsed from hands, it only kills pathogens and does nothing to remove organic matter. So, hands "cleaned" with hand sanitizer may still harbor pathogens. Thus, while hand sanitizer can be helpful in situations where soap and clean water isn't available, a simple hand washing is still the best option.

1. Knowing that the temperature of the water does not affect the efficacy of hand washing, one can conclude that water plays an important role in hand washing because it

    A) has antibacterial properties.

    B) physically removes pathogens from hands.

    C) cools hands to make them inhospitable to dangerous bacteria.

    D) is hot enough to kill bacteria.

2. What is the meaning of the word *harbor* in the last paragraph?

    A) to disguise

    B) to hide

    C) to wash away

    D) to give a home

3. Which of the following is NOT a fact stated in the passage?

   A) Many infections occur because people get pathogens on their hands and then touch their own eyes, mouths, or noses.

   B) Antibacterial soaps and warm water are the best way to remove pathogens from hands.

   C) Most hand sanitizers have a concentration of at least 60 percent alcohol.

   D) Hand sanitizer can be an acceptable alternative to hand washing when soap and water aren't available.

4. What is the best summary of this passage?

   A) Many diseases are spread by pathogens that can live on the hands. Hand washing is the best way to remove these pathogens and prevent disease.

   B) Simple hand washing can prevent the spread of many common illnesses, including the flu, the common cold, diarrhea, and many acute respiratory illnesses. Hand sanitizer can also kill the pathogens that cause these diseases.

   C) Simple hand washing with soap and cold water is an effective way to reduce the spread of disease. Antibacterial soaps and hand sanitizers may also be used but are not significantly more effective.

   D) Using hand sanitizer will kill many pathogens but will not remove organic matter. Hand washing with soap and water is a better option when available.

5. What is the author's primary purpose in writing this essay?

   A) to persuade readers of the importance and effectiveness of hand washing with soap and cold water

   B) to dissuade readers from using hand sanitizer

   C) to explain how many common diseases are spread through daily interaction

   D) to describe the many ways hand washing and hand sanitizer provide health benefits

6. What can the reader conclude from the passage above?

   A) Hand washing would do little to limit infections that spread through particles in the air.

   B) Hand washing is not necessary for people who do not touch their eyes, mouths, or noses with their hands.

   C) Hand sanitizer serves no purpose and should not be used as an alternative to hand washing.

   D) Hand sanitizer will likely soon replace hand washing as the preferred method of removing pathogens from hands.

Questions 7–12 refer to the following passage.

The bacteria, fungi, insects, plants, and animals that live together in a habitat have evolved to share a pool of limited resources. They've competed for water, minerals, nutrients, sunlight, and space—sometimes for thousands or even millions of years. As these communities have evolved, the species in them have developed complex, long-term interspecies interactions known as symbiotic relationships.

Ecologists characterize these interactions based on whether each party benefits. In mutualism, both individuals benefit, while in synnecrosis, both organisms are harmed. A relationship where one individual benefits and the other is harmed is known as parasitism. Examples of these relationships can easily be seen in any ecosystem. Pollination, for example, is mutualistic—pollinators get nutrients from the flower, and the plant is able to reproduce—while tapeworms, which steal nutrients from their host, are parasitic.

There's yet another class of symbiosis that is controversial among scientists. As it's long been defined, commensalism is a relationship where one species benefits and the other is unaffected. But is it possible for two species to interact and for one to remain completely unaffected? Often, relationships described as commensal include one species that feeds on another species' leftovers; remoras, for instance, will attach themselves to sharks and eat the food particles they leave behind. It might seem like the shark gets nothing from the relationship, but a closer look will show that sharks in fact benefit from remoras, which clean the sharks' skin and remove parasites. In fact, many scientists claim that relationships currently described as commensal are just mutualistic or parasitic in ways that haven't been discovered yet.

7. What is the author's primary purpose in writing this essay?

  A) to argue that commensalism isn't actually found in nature

  B) to describe the many types of symbiotic relationships

  C) to explain how competition for resources results in long-term interspecies relationships

  D) to provide examples of the many different ways individual organisms interact

8. Which of the following is NOT a fact stated in the passage?

  A) Mutualism is an interspecies relationship where both species benefit.

  B) Synnecrosis is an interspecies relationship where both species are harmed.

  C) The relationship between plants and pollinators is mutualistic.

  D) The relationship between remoras and sharks is parasitic.

9. Epiphytes are plants that attach themselves to trees and derive nutrients from the air and surrounding debris. Sometimes, the weight of epiphytes can damage the trees on which they're growing. The relationship between epiphytes and their hosts would be described as

  A) mutualism.

  B) commensalism.

  C) parasitism.

  D) synnecrosis.

10. What is the meaning of the word *controversial* in the last paragraph?

  A) debatable

  B) objectionable

  C) confusing

  D) upsetting

11. Why is commensalism controversial among scientists?

  A) Many scientists believe that an interspecies interaction where one species is unaffected does not exist.

  B) Some scientists believe that relationships where one species feeds on the leftovers of another should be classified as parasitism.

  C) Because remoras and sharks have a mutualistic relationship, no interactions should be classified as commensalism.

  D) Only relationships among animal species should be classified as commensalism.

12. What can the reader conclude from this passage about symbiotic relationships?

  A) Scientists cannot decide how to classify symbiotic relationships among species.

  B) The majority of interspecies interactions are parasitic because most species do not get along.

  C) If two species are involved in a parasitic relationship, one of the species will eventually become extinct.

  D) Symbiotic relationships evolve as the species that live in a community adapt to their environments and each other.

Questions 13–18 refer to the following passage.

Influenza (also called the flu) has historically been one of the most common, and deadliest, human infections. While many people who contract the virus will recover, many others will not. Over the past 150 years, tens of millions of people have died from the flu, and millions more have been left with lingering complications such as secondary infections.

Although it's a common disease, the flu is not actually highly infectious, meaning it's relatively difficult to contract. The flu can only be transmitted when individuals come into direct contact with bodily fluids of people infected with the flu or when they are exposed to expelled aerosol particles (which result from coughing and sneezing). Because the viruses can only travel short distances as aerosol particles and will die within a few hours on hard surfaces, the virus can be contained with fairly simple health measures like hand washing and face masks.

However, the spread of the flu can only be contained when people are aware such measures need to be taken. One of the reasons the flu has historically been so deadly is the amount of time between when people become infectious and when they develop symptoms. Viral shedding—the process by which the body releases viruses that have been successfully reproducing during the infection—takes place two days after infection, while symptoms do not usually develop until the third day of infection. Thus, infected individuals have at least twenty-four hours in which they may unknowingly infect others.

13. What is the main idea of the passage?
   A) The flu is a deadly disease that's difficult to control because people become infectious before they show symptoms.
   B) For the flu to be transmitted, individuals must come in contact with bodily fluids from infected individuals.
   C) The spread of the flu is easy to contain because the viruses do not live long either as aerosol particles or on hard surfaces.
   D) The flu has killed tens of millions of people and can often cause deadly secondary infections.

14. Which of the following correctly describes the flu?
   A) The flu is easy to contract and always fatal.
   B) The flu is difficult to contract and always fatal.
   C) The flu is easy to contract and sometimes fatal.
   D) The flu is difficult to contract and sometimes fatal.

15. Why is the flu considered to not be highly infectious?
   A) Many people who get the flu will recover and have no lasting complications, so only a small number of people who become infected will die.
   B) The process of viral shedding takes two days, so infected individuals have enough time to implement simple health measures that stop the spread of the disease.
   C) The flu virus cannot travel far or live for long periods of time outside the human body, so its spread can easily be contained.

   D) Twenty-four hours is a relatively short period of time for the virus to spread among a population.

16. What is the meaning of the word *measures* in the last paragraph?
   A) a plan of action
   B) a standard unit
   C) an adequate amount
   D) a rhythmic movement

17. Which statement is NOT a detail from the passage?
   A) Tens of millions of people have been killed by the flu virus.
   B) There is typically a twenty-four-hour window during which individuals are infectious but not showing flu symptoms.
   C) Viral shedding is the process by which people recover from the flu.
   D) The flu can be transmitted by direct contact with bodily fluids from infected individuals or by exposure to aerosol particles.

18. What can the reader conclude from the previous passage?
   A) Preemptively implementing health measures like hand washing and face masks could help stop the spread of the flu virus.
   B) Doctors are not sure how the flu virus is transmitted, so they are unsure how to stop it from spreading.
   C) The flu is dangerous because it is both deadly and highly infectious.
   D) Individuals stop being infectious three days after they are infected.

Questions 19–24 refer to the following passage.

Across the globe, women are, on average, outliving their male counterparts. Although this gender gap has shrunk over the last decade thanks to medical improvements and lifestyle changes, women are still expected to live four and a half years longer than men. What is the reason for this trend? The answer may lie in our sex hormones.

Men are more likely to exhibit riskier behaviors than women, especially between the ages of fifteen and twenty-four, when testosterone production is at its peak. Testosterone is correlated with aggressive and reckless behaviors that contribute to high mortality rates—think road rage, alcohol consumption, drug use, and smoking.

Estrogen, on the other hand, seems to be correlated with cholesterol levels: an increase in estrogen is accompanied by a decrease in "bad" cholesterol, which may confer advantages by reducing the risk of heart attack and stroke.

Of course, lifestyle and diet are also components of this difference in life expectancy. Men are more likely to be involved in more physically dangerous jobs, such as manufacturing or construction. They may be less likely to eat as many fruits and vegetables as their female counterparts. And they may be more likely to consume more red meat, including processed meat. These types of meats have been linked to high cholesterol, hypertension, and cancer. Better health decisions and better nutrition may eventually even the score in men's and women's life expectancy.

19. What does the second paragraph mainly concern?

   A) testosterone production
   B) young men's behavior
   C) reasons why some men die young
   D) reasons why women outlive men

20. What is the author's primary purpose in writing this essay?

   A) to warn men to stop behaving riskily and eating unhealthy foods
   B) to explain why, on average, women today outlive men
   C) to advise readers about ways to extend life expectancy
   D) to express the hope that men's life expectancy will go up

21. Which of the following statements can be considered a statement of FACT according to the content offered in the paragraphs above?

   A) Sex hormones are the sole cause of the gender gap in life expectancy.
   B) Women's diets are better than men's, so women are slimmer and live longer.
   C) Because of risky behavior, most men die before they reach middle age.
   D) Worldwide, the average woman lives four and a half years longer than the average man.

22. According to the passage, what is true about women and men?

   A) In general, women care more about life expectancy than men do.
   B) In general, men care more about having fun than women do.
   C) In general, women take better care of themselves than men do.
   D) In general, men's bodies contain more sex hormones than women's do.

23. Readers can infer that in the past decade, men have been

   A) engaging in riskier behavior.
   B) eating more red meat.
   C) making positive lifestyle changes.
   D) visiting their primary care doctors more often.

24. What is the meaning of the word *correlated* in the third paragraph?

   A) associated
   B) incompatible
   C) isolated
   D) mismatched

Questions 25–30 refer to the following passage.

The discovery of penicillin by Alexander Fleming in 1928 revolutionized medical care. The widespread use of penicillin and other antibiotics has saved millions of people from the deadliest bacterial infections known to humans and prevented the spread of bacterial diseases. But we have relied on antibiotics too heavily, which has undermined their effectiveness as bacteria evolve resistance to these drugs.

To add to the problem, factory farms across the United States are inundating pigs, cattle, chickens, and turkeys with cocktails of antibiotics to prevent diseases from proliferating among their tightly packed livestock. Because livestock manure is used as fertilizer, drug-resistant bacteria are spreading within the soils and waterways of farms, contaminating even plant-producing environments. The result: a dramatic rise in drug-resistant bacterial infections, sickening two million people per year and killing 23,000 in the United States alone.

25. Which sentence best summarizes the passage's main idea?

   A) "The discovery of penicillin by Alexander Fleming in 1928 revolutionized medical care."

   B) "The widespread use of penicillin and other antibiotics has saved millions of people from the deadliest bacterial infections known to humans and prevented the spread of bacterial diseases."

   C) "But we have relied on antibiotics too heavily, which has undermined their effectiveness as bacteria evolve resistance to these drugs."

   D) "Because livestock manure is used as fertilizer, drug-resistant bacteria are spreading within the soils and waterways of farms, contaminating even plant-producing environments."

26. What is the meaning of the word *revolutionized* in the first sentence?

   A) rebelled and rejected authority

   B) protested unfair treatment

   C) inspired hopeful thoughts

   D) transformed and modernized

27. Which of the following is NOT listed as a detail in the passage?

   A) Factory farms give antibiotics to pigs, cattle, chickens, and turkeys.

   B) Factory farmers give their animals "cocktails of antibiotics"—more than one kind of antibiotics.

   C) On factory farms, livestock are packed closely together.

   D) On some farms, free-range chickens and turkeys can wander about the property.

28. What is the author's primary purpose in writing this essay?

   A) to suggest changing the ways we use antibiotics

   B) to suggest that people need to stop taking so many antibiotics

   C) to honor Alexander Fleming's groundbreaking discovery of penicillin

   D) to suggest that factory farmers need to start treating their animals more humanely

29. Readers can infer from reading this passage that the author feels _____ about the "dramatic rise in drug-resistant bacterial infections."

   A) relieved

   B) concerned

   C) infuriated

   D) enthralled

30. In the last sentence, what does the word *dramatic* mean?

   A) theatrical

   B) impressive

   C) thrilling

   D) striking

VERBAL ABILITY

Synonyms

DIRECTIONS: Choose the word that is the closest in meaning.

1. *Amalgam* most nearly means:
   A) blend
   B) process
   C) schedule
   D) conference

2. *Adhere* most nearly means:
   A) follow
   B) reject
   C) uphold
   D) interpret

3. *Deleterious* most nearly means:
   A) helpful
   B) harmful
   C) gentle
   D) constructive

4. *Prone* most nearly means:
   A) excited
   B) flat
   C) unconscious
   D) uncomfortable

5. *Ambulatory* most nearly means:
   A) healthy
   B) recovered
   C) symptomatic
   D) walking

6. *Superficial* most nearly means:
   A) shallow
   B) impressive
   C) gruesome
   D) jagged

7. *Malaise* most nearly means:
   A) nausea
   B) headache
   C) unease
   D) vomiting

8. *Respiration* most nearly means:
   A) breathing
   B) sleeping
   C) digestion
   D) heartbeat

9. *Transient* most nearly means:
   A) repetitive
   B) severe
   C) extreme
   D) temporary

10. *Incompatible* most nearly means:
    A) friendly
    B) cooperative
    C) mismatched
    D) talkative

11. *Transmit* most nearly means:
    A) treat
    B) study
    C) pass on
    D) eliminate

12. *Void* most nearly means:
    A) ease
    B) strengthen
    C) empty
    D) feel

13. *Therapeutic* most nearly means:
    A) healing
    B) prescribed
    C) systemic
    D) targeted

14. *Discreet* most nearly means:
    A) careful
    B) accurate
    C) loud
    D) exact

15. *Abstain* most nearly means:

    A) ingest

    B) resist

    C) refrain

    D) intake

Sentence Clarity

DIRECTIONS: Read the question carefully, and then choose the most correct answer.

16. Which of the following sentences is grammatically correct?

    A) Kiana went to class; but Lara stayed home.

    B) Kiana went to class, but Lara stayed home.

    C) Kiana went to class, Lara stayed home though.

    D) Kiana went to class but Lara stayed home.

17. Which of the following sentences is grammatically correct?

    A) You can take either the bus nor the subway.

    B) You can't take neither the bus nor the subway.

    C) You can take either the bus or the subway.

    D) You can taking either the bus or the subway.

18. Which of the following sentences is grammatically correct?

    A) If Pablo studies diligently, Pablo will probably do good on the test.

    B) If Pablo studies diligently, he will probably do well on the test.

    C) If Pablo studies diligently, he will probably do good on the test.

    D) If Pablo studies diligent, he will probably do well on the test.

19. Which of the following sentences is grammatically correct?

    A) One of my teammates hope to be the star player tonight.

    B) Two of my teammates hopes to be star players tonight.

    C) All my teammates hopes to play their best tonight.

    D) Of course, no one on our team wants to play poorly.

20. Which of the following sentences is grammatically correct?

    A) They are standing right over they're with their brother.

    B) They're standing right over their with there brother.

    C) Their standing right over there with their brother.

    D) They're standing right over there with their brother.

21. Which of the following sentences is grammatically correct?

    A) Inmates received lunches in bags from deputies.

    B) Inmates received lunches from deputies in bags.

    C) Deputies offered lunches to be distributed by inmates in bags.

    D) Deputies received lunches from inmates in bags.

22. Which of the following sentences uses capitalization correctly?

    A) My aunt, my Mom's sister, lives in British Columbia, Canada, with her Husband.

    B) My aunt, my mom's sister, lives in British Columbia, Canada, with her husband.

    C) My Aunt, my mom's sister, lives in British columbia, Canada, with her husband.

    D) My Aunt, my Mom's sister, lives in British Columbia, Canada, with her Husband.

23. Which of the following sentences is grammatically correct?

    A) Alexa is the smartest of the three sisters.

    B) Alexa is the smarter of the three sisters.

    C) Alexa is the most smart of the three sisters.

    D) Alexa is more smart than her two sisters.

24. Which of the following sentences is grammatically correct?

A) Brenda and Pauletta are working late because the deadline was tomorrow.

B) Brenda and Pauletta were working late because the deadline was tomorrow.

C) Brenda and Pauletta are working late because the deadline is tomorrow.

D) Brenda and Pauletta is working late because the deadline is tomorrow.

25. Which of the following choices uses punctuation correctly?

A) My cat Katrina isn't the only female in our home, there's Hollie the dog, and I am female, too.

B) My cat Katrina isnt the only female in our home: theres Hollie the dog, and I am female, too.

C) My cat Katrina isn't the only female in our home: there's Hollie the dog, and I am female, too.

D) My cat Katrina isnt' the only female in our home? There's Hollie the dog, and I am female, too.

26. Which of the following sentences is grammatically correct?

A) On Monday, either my sisters or our parents picks me up at the bus station.

B) On Monday, either my sisters or our parents pick me up at the bus station.

C) On Monday, either my sisters nor our parents pick me up at the bus station.

D) On Monday, neither my sisters or our parents pick me up at the bus station.

27. Which version of the sentence is most clear and correct?

A) Mario realized he had burned the soup by leaving it on the stove for too long.

B) Left on the stove for too long, Mario realized he had burned the soup.

C) Burning on the stove, Mario realized he had left the soup on for too long.

D) Realizing that Mario had burned it, the soup stayed on the stove for too long.

28. Which of the following sentences is grammatically correct?

A) The cat eat their food while the dog sleep in their bed.

B) The cats eats its food while the dog sleep in their bed.

C) The cat eat their food while the dogs sleep in their bed.

D) The cat eats its food while the dogs sleep in their beds.

29. Which of the following sentences uses capitalization correctly?

A) The Automobile industry earned more than Microsoft did last year.

B) The automobile industry earned more than microsoft did last year.

C) The Automobile Industry earned more than Microsoft did last year.

D) The automobile industry earned more than Microsoft did last year.

30. Which of the following sentences is grammatically correct?

A) My teacher and the school principal has worked together for many years.

B) My teacher and the school principal have worked together for many years.

C) My teacher and the school principal have been worked together for many years.

D) My teacher and the school principal had working together for many years.

31. Which of the following sentences uses punctuation correctly?

A) My cat (Jack) likes the following items in this order, food, affection, and lying in the sunlight.

B) My cat Jack likes the following items in this order; food, affection, and lying in the sunlight.

C) My cat Jack likes the following items in this order: food, affection, and lying in the sunlight.

D) My cat Jack likes the following items in this order: food, affection, and lying in the sunlight?

32. Which version of the sentence is most clear and correct?

    A) Everyone want to succeed in business.

    B) Everybody want to succeed in business.

    C) None of us wants to owe a lot of money.

    D) Nobody want to owe a lot of money to the bank.

33. Which version of the sentence is most clear and correct?

    A) DeQuan loves eating pizza, but meat toppings make him feel queasy.

    B) Though he avoids meat toppings, pizza is one of DeQuan's favorite foods.

    C) Meat toppings on pizza makes DeQuan feel queasy.

    D) Pizza is one of DeQuan's favorite foods but he can't put meat on it.

34. Which of the following sentences uses capitalization correctly?

    A) There are many Oceans on our planet; the Pacific and the Atlantic are the two largest.

    B) There are many oceans on our Planet; the pacific and the Atlantic are the two largest.

    C) There are many oceans on our planet; the Pacific and the Atlantic are the two largest.

    D) There are many Oceans on our Planet; the Pacific and the Atlantic are the two Largest.

35. Which of the following sentences is grammatically correct?

    A) Of my two parents, Dad is the most old.

    B) Of my two parents, Dad is more older.

    C) Of my two parents, Dad is older.

    D) Of my two parents, Dad is the oldest.

Spelling

DIRECTIONS: Select the choice that reflects the correct spelling of the word. If none are correct, choose "none of the above."

36.
    A) tward
    B) toword
    C) toward
    D) none of the above

37.
    A) liaison
    B) liason
    C) laison
    D) none of the above

38.
    A) resinded
    B) recinded
    C) rescinded
    D) none of the above

39.
    A) surprised
    B) suprised
    C) supprised
    D) none of the above

40.
    A) tendancy
    B) tendency
    C) tendincy
    D) none of the above

41.
    A) necessary
    B) nesisarry
    C) necissary
    D) none of the above

42.
    A) goverment
    B) govermant
    C) govirnment
    D) none of the above

43.
    A) acomodations
    B) accommodations
    C) accommadations
    D) none of the above

44.
- A) harassing
- B) harrassing
- C) harasing
- D) none of the above

45.
- A) noticably
- B) noticibly
- C) noticeably
- D) none of the above

46.
- A) posession
- B) possesion
- C) possession
- D) none of the above

47.
- A) siege
- B) seige
- C) seege
- D) none of the above

48.
- A) publicly
- B) publicely
- C) publicaly
- D) none of the above

49.
- A) agresive
- B) aggresive
- C) agressive
- D) none of the above

50.
- A) floresent
- B) fluorescent
- C) flourescent
- D) none of the above

51.
- A) adversarial
- B) advirsarial
- C) advirsareal
- D) none of the above

52.
- A) germain
- B) germean
- C) germane
- D) none of the above

53.
- A) palpible
- B) palpable
- C) palpebal
- D) none of the above

54.
- A) supena
- B) suppena
- C) subpoena
- D) none of the above

55.
- A) suspisious
- B) suspicious
- C) suspiscious
- D) none of the above

Verbal Analogies

DIRECTIONS: Complete the sentence such that the relationship expressed in the first set of words is duplicated in the second set.

56. Comedy is to tragedy as joy is to
- A) calamity.
- B) joke.
- C) fury.
- D) desperation.

57. Run is to walk as fast is to
- A) quick.
- B) slow.
- C) hurry.
- D) turtle.

58. Stop is to sign as traffic is to
    A) slow.
    B) stop.
    C) yield.
    D) light.

59. Frantic is to desperate as angry is to
    A) happy.
    B) energetic.
    C) irate.
    D) cool.

60. Cup is to mug as trophy is to
    A) beaker.
    B) prize.
    C) demitasse.
    D) weight.

61. Cookie is to chocolate chips as pizza is to
    A) oven.
    B) yeast.
    C) pepperoni.
    D) delicious.

62. Recreation is to amusement as exhaustion is to
    A) hobby.
    B) restoration.
    C) work.
    D) fatigue.

63. Puzzle is to piece as team is to
    A) referee.
    B) player.
    C) soccer.
    D) base.

64. Feather is to bird as fur is to
    A) frog.
    B) dog.
    C) penguin.
    D) turkey.

65. Tree is to forest as bird is to
    A) flock.
    B) nest.
    C) feather.
    D) flight.

66. Train is to rail as car is to
    A) path.
    B) sidewalk.
    C) road.
    D) parking.

67. String is to guitar as lace is to
    A) coat.
    B) shoe.
    C) plant.
    D) rug.

68. Foghorn is to lighthouse as siren is to
    A) firetruck.
    B) school.
    C) alarm.
    D) weather.

69. Log is to fireplace as shovel is to
    A) pitchfork.
    B) tool.
    C) dirt.
    D) garden.

70. Flowerpot is to houseplant as pan is to
    A) sink.
    B) brownies.
    C) stove.
    D) cabinet.

Vocabulary

DIRECTIONS: Choose the word closest in meaning to the given word.

71. SUBTLE most nearly means:

A) obvious

B) rapid

C) slight

D) large

72. INNOCUOUS most nearly means:

A) glamorous

B) healthy

C) harmless

D) worrisome

73. AMALGAM most nearly means:

A) blend

B) process

C) schedule

D) conference

74. ADVERSELY most nearly means:

A) consequently

B) harmfully

C) helpfully

D) expectedly

75. POTENT most nearly means:

A) powerful

B) weak

C) detrimental

D) nutritional

76. ASYMMETRIC most nearly means:

A) patterned

B) unbalanced

C) circular

D) aligned

77. SUCCUMBED most nearly means:

A) ignored

B) fought

C) surrendered

D) enjoyed

78. EXCESSIVE most nearly means:

A) too many

B) a variety of

C) prescribed by a doctor

D) taken orally

79. SENSIBLE most nearly means:

A) confusing

B) prohibited

C) necessary

D) wise

80. JUSTIFY most nearly means:

A) understand

B) explain

C) organize

D) introduce

81. REGRESS most nearly means:

A) got better

B) strengthened

C) worsened

D) failed

82. PRAGMATIC most nearly means:

A) practical

B) logical

C) emotional

D) aloof

83. RETAIN most nearly means:

A) excrete

B) shed

C) filter

D) hold

84. DYSFUNCTIONAL most nearly means:

A) vast

B) expensive

C) intricate

D) flawed

85. DIMINISH most nearly means:
   A) identify
   B) decrease
   C) stop
   D) intensify

86. ACCOUNTABILITY most nearly means:
   A) responsibility
   B) accuracy
   C) compliance
   D) confidence

87. ABBREVIATE most nearly means:
   A) lengthen
   B) avoid
   C) extend
   D) shorten

88. COHORT most nearly means:
   A) colleague
   B) acquaintance
   C) group
   D) associate

89. BENIGN most nearly means:
   A) symptomatic
   B) harmful
   C) harmless
   D) detrimental

90. CONSISTENCY most nearly means:
   A) irregularity
   B) precision
   C) mistakes
   D) uniformity

Improve a Passage

DIRECTIONS: Read this passage; some portions of the passage are underlined and numbered. Read the questions that correspond to the underlined portions of the text, and choose the best way to fix errors in the underlined portion. If no changes are needed, select NO CHANGE. Some questions ask about the effectiveness of the text, whether wording should be added, or whether the writer has fulfilled their goal.

Across the United States, a new trend in dining has taken (91)hold. Cities like Austin, Portland, San Francisco, and Seattle are seeing a significant increase in one particular type of dining establishment—the food truck. Though the modern food truck phenomenon is still in (92)it's prime, mobile dining is in no way (93)a unique, novel idea: precursors to the modern food truck can be traced back as far as the 1800s.

The earliest predecessors to the modern food truck (94)was actually not trucks; in fact, they were not motorized at all. (95)Push carts were some of the earliest vehicles for mobile food distribution and were popular in urban areas like New York City, where workers needed access to quick, cheap lunches. (96)Instead, while these carts were mobile, (97)they were not always available when they were most needed.

In the late 1800s, two new inventions marked important milestones in the development of the modern food truck. In 1866, Charles Goodnight created the first (98)chuck wagon and a covered wagon that served as a mobile kitchen for cowmen who were herding cattle northward for sale. The cooks, or "cookies," who traveled with the cowmen would wake early and prepare meals of beans, dried meats, and biscuits using the tools and ingredients on the chuck wagon. (99) Similarly, in 1872, a food vendor named Walter Scott conceived of the lunch wagon, from which he would serve sandwiches, coffee, and desserts to journalists outside a Providence, Rhode Island, newspaper office.

[1] In the 1900s, mobile dining took even newer forms, as the invention of motorized transportation began to transform the industry. [2] Ice cream trucks followed in the 1950s, serving children and adults alike cold treats on hot summer afternoons. [3] In the 1960s, large food service trucks called roach coaches began to pop up near densely populated urban areas, often serving cheap meals from grungy kitchens. (100) (101)

(102)In recent years, the food truck industry has transformed the mobile dining experience from one of convenience to one of excitement. Today, city dwellers and tourists (103)will have flocked to food trucks not only for ease and affordability, but also for unique foods, new flavors, and fun experiences. In some places, whole streets or even neighborhoods are devoted to hosting these food trucks, (104)so they are easier than ever to access. (105)

91.

A) NO CHANGE

B) hold in cities

C) hold of cities

D) hold, cities

92.

A) NO CHANGE

B) its

C) its'

D) it is

93.

A) NO CHANGE

B) a new or novel idea

C) a novel idea

D) a uniquely novel idea

94.

A) NO CHANGE

B) were

C) are

D) is

95.

A) NO CHANGE

B) Push carts were some of the earliest vehicles for mobile food distribution, popular in urban areas where workers needed access to quick, cheap lunches like New York City.

C) Popular in urban areas like New York City, some of the earliest vehicles for mobile food distribution were push carts, which were located wherever workers needed access to quick, cheap lunches.

D) Some of the earliest vehicles were push carts for food distribution, popular in urban areas, like New York, where workers needed quick, cheap lunches in the city.

96.

A) NO CHANGE

B) However,

C) As a result,

D) Therefore,

97. Given that all of the choices are true, which of the following would be most effective in highlighting one of the major differences between the push cart and the modern food truck?

A) NO CHANGE

B) they sometimes stayed in one place for long periods of time.

C) they were not equipped with the tools necessary to prepare the food.

D) they often had the same people working in them all the time.

98.

A) NO CHANGE

B) chuck wagon, and a covered wagon

C) chuck wagon, a covered wagon

D) chuck wagon; a covered wagon

99. If the writer were to delete the preceding sentence, the paragraph would primarily lose

A) details about how cooks on the cattle trails came to be called cookies.

B) a transition between two points in the paragraph.

C) details about how the cooks made food on the chuck wagons.

D) information about the meaning of the phrase *mobile kitchen.*

100. The writer is considering deleting the words *cheap* and *grungy* from the preceding sentence. Should the writer make these deletions?

  A) Yes, because the words distract from the main idea of the sentence.

  B) Yes, because the words are offensive to people who like food trucks.

  C) No, because the words provide insight into the origin of the term *roach coach*.

  D) No, because the words provide more information about early food trucks.

101. Upon reviewing the previous paragraph and realizing that some information had been left out, the writer composes the following sentence:

During the World War II era, mobile canteens popped up near army bases to serve quick, easy meals to the troops.

The most logical placement for this sentence would be

  A) before sentence 1.

  B) before sentence 2.

  C) before sentence 3.

  D) after sentence 3.

102.

  A) NO CHANGE

  B) Consequently,

  C) Therefore,

  D) In conclusion,

103.

  A) NO CHANGE

  B) are flocking

  C) have flocked

  D) have been flocking

104. Which of the following choices would provide an ending most consistent with the statement made in the first sentence of the paragraph?

  A) NO CHANGE

  B) so you rarely run out of delicious options.

  C) but sometimes these areas can be busy.

  D) and people travel from all over the city, sometimes even farther, to try what they're offering.

105. Suppose the writer had intended to write an essay on the historical development of the modern food truck. Would this essay successfully fulfill that goal?

  A) Yes, because it provides detailed information about the inventor who designed the first food truck.

  B) Yes, because it provides a brief overview of the trends and innovations that preceded the modern food truck.

  C) No, because it is primarily a descriptive essay about the modern food truck trend and its followers.

  D) No, because it focuses primarily on the differences between modern food trucks and older forms of mobile food distribution.

Visual Analogies

DIRECTIONS: Choose the shape that correctly completes the statement.

106.

  A) ▽ B) ⬖ C) ⬗ D) ▥

107. M is to ◁ as Ϛ is to ?

  A) △ B) ▽ C) ◗ D) ◁

108. ⬡ is to ⬢ as △ is to ?

  A) ● B) ▲ C) ■ D) ◀

109. ◔ is to ◓ as ◕ is to ?

  A) ◶ B) ◕ C) ◔ D) ◖

110.

  A) ⣿ B) ⣿ C) ⣿ D) ⣿

111. ⊟ is to ⊟ as ⊟ is to ?

  A)   B)   C)   D)

112. ▯|||| is to |▯||| as |||▯| is to ?

A) ||▯|| B) ▯|||| C) |||▯| D) ||||▯

113. ⊔| is to ⊔|| as ⊢ is to ?

A) Ⅎ B) ⊨ C) Ε D) Ϝ

114. 8 is to 8 as 8 is to ?

A) 8 B) 8 C) 8 D) 8

115. ⊵ is to ◣ as ◤ is to ?

A) ◸ B) ◿ C) ◢ D) ◹

MATHEMATICS

DIRECTIONS: Work the problem, and then choose the most correct answer.

1. $(-9)(-4) =$
   - A) -13
   - B) 13
   - C) -36
   - D) 36

2. A box of books weighs 6.3 pounds. If there are 18 books in the box, how much does each book weigh?
   - A) 1.134 lb
   - B) 11.7 lb
   - C) 0.35 lb
   - D) 3.5 lb

3. Andre welded together three pieces of metal pipe, measuring 26.5 inches, 18.9 inches, and 35.1 inches. How long was the welded pipe?
   - A) 10.3 in
   - B) 80.5 in
   - C) 27.5 in
   - D) 42.7 in

4. John's rain gauge recorded rain on three consecutive days: $\frac{1}{2}$ inch on Sunday, $\frac{2}{3}$ inch on Monday, and $\frac{1}{4}$ inch on Tuesday. What was the total amount of rain received over the three days?
   - A) $\frac{17}{36}$ in
   - B) $1\frac{5}{12}$ in
   - C) $\frac{4}{9}$ in
   - D) $1\frac{1}{2}$ in

5. Solve the proportion: $\frac{5}{x} = \frac{7}{14}$
   - A) 70
   - B) 10
   - C) 2.5
   - D) 25

6. What is 40% of 124?
   - A) 310
   - B) 4.96
   - C) 49.6
   - D) 31

7. Solve: $12x + 5 = 77$
   - A) -6
   - B) 6
   - C) 10
   - D) 8

8. $-48 \div (-6) =$
   - A) -8
   - B) 8
   - C) 7
   - D) 6

9. An employee is given $100 petty cash to purchase 6 binders and 6 sets of dividers at the office supply store. Divider sets are $3.49 each, and the binders come in packages of two for $10.49 per package. How much money will the employee return to petty cash?
   - A) $52.41
   - B) $16.12
   - C) $83.88
   - D) $47.59

10. Danika bought two packages of ground beef weighing 1.73 pounds and 2.17 pounds. What was the total weight of the two packages?
    - A) 0.44 lb
    - B) 3.81 lb
    - C) 3.9 lb
    - D) 4.2 lb

11. Alice ran $3\frac{1}{2}$ miles on Monday, and she increased her distance by $\frac{1}{4}$ mile each day. What was her total distance from Monday to Friday?
    - A) $17\frac{1}{2}$ mi
    - B) 20 mi
    - C) $18\frac{1}{2}$ mi
    - D) 19 mi

12. A food label says that the box holds 2.5 servings. How many boxes would be needed to provide 10 servings?

    A) 4 boxes

    B) 25 boxes

    C) 10 boxes

    D) 6 boxes

13. 26 is 40% of what number?

    A) 65

    B) 10.4

    C) 66

    D) 650

14. Angelica bought a roast weighing 3.2 pounds. If the roast cost $25.44, how much did it cost per pound?

    A) $5.95

    B) $7.95

    C) $7.44

    D) $8.14

15. $4 - (-20) =$

    A) −16

    B) −24

    C) 24

    D) 16

16. Simplify the following expression:

    $9^2 + 2(7^2 - 1)$

    A) 3984

    B) 44

    C) 177

    D) 260

17. $75.00 − $39.73

    A) $36.73

    B) $46.27

    C) $44.73

    D) $35.27

18. How much alcohol by volume is in a 500 milliliter bottle of 70% isopropyl alcohol?

    A) 35 ml

    B) 50 ml

    C) 400 ml

    D) 350 ml

19. Kenna lost an average of 1.1 pounds per week for an entire year. How much weight did she lose? (Round to the nearest whole number.)

    A) 47 lb

    B) 53 lb

    C) 46 lb

    D) 57 lb

20. The recommended dosage of a particular medication is 4 milliliters per 50 pounds of body weight. What is the recommended dosage for a person who weighs 175 pounds?

    A) 25 ml

    B) 140 ml

    C) 14 ml

    D) 28 ml

21. If $285.48 will be shared equally by six people, how much will each person receive?

    A) $1712.88

    B) $47.58

    C) $885.46

    D) $225.48

22. A bank account is $20 overdrawn. The bank charges the customer a $25 overdraft fee. What is the bank account balance now?

    A) −$5

    B) $15

    C) $5

    D) −$45

23. Simplify the following expression:

    $(9 + 6) \times (2 - 5)$

    A) −45

    B) 45

    C) 25

    D) 16

24. When Darlene left the house on Monday morning, the odometer in her car read 66,284.8. After work on Friday, it read 66,653.2. How many miles did she drive that week?

    A) 368.4 mi

    B) 431.6 mi

    C) 36.84 mi

    D) 479.5 mi

25. Chris makes $13.50 an hour. How much will he earn in a 7.5-hour day?

    A) $101.25
    B) $1012.50
    C) $20.75
    D) $91.00

26. The ratio of men to women in a school program is 2 to 7. If there are 72 men in the program, how many women are there?

    A) 504 women
    B) 21 women
    C) 252 women
    D) 210 women

27. In a class of 25 students, four students were absent. What percent of the students were absent?

    A) 4%
    B) 16%
    C) 21%
    D) 84%

28. Solve: $-4x + 2 = -34$

    A) 8
    B) −8
    C) −9
    D) 9

29. In their first year of business, a small company lost $2100. The next year, the company recorded a profit of $11,200. What was the company's average profit over the two years?

    A) $5650
    B) $4550
    C) $9100
    D) $11,300

30. Juan is packing a shipment of three books weighing 0.8 pounds, 0.49 pounds, and 0.89 pounds. The maximum weight for the shipping box is 2.5 pounds. How much more weight will the box hold?

    A) 2.18 lb
    B) 0.32 lb
    C) 0.48 lb
    D) 4.68 lb

CLERICAL SKILLS

Alphabetization

DIRECTIONS: Insert the word into the correct alphabetical position in the list. Choose the letter of the word it precedes.

1. FIGHTERS
   A) fifty
   B) finite
   C) fitting
   D) fizzled

2. VICTOR
   A) vicious
   B) victim
   C) Vincent
   D) violent

3. PRORATED
   A) professional
   B) promises
   C) proper
   D) protest

4. OBLONG
   A) object
   B) obligate
   C) obnoxious
   D) obsession

5. ADJACENT
   A) adjective
   B) adjoint
   C) adjourn
   D) adjust

6. HYDRATE
   A) hydration
   B) hydrogen
   C) hydroplane
   D) hydroxy

7. WHISKERS
   A) where
   B) whining
   C) whimpers
   D) whispers

8. BICYCLE
   A) biclops
   B) binoculars
   C) biography
   D) bionic

9. GIGANTIC
   A) giant
   B) gigabyte
   C) gingerly
   D) ginormous

10. BEACH
    A) bell
    B) Bennington
    C) Bering
    D) Beverly

11. EXCISE
    A) excite
    B) execute
    C) exercise
    D) expire

12. KNIGHT
    A) kneeling
    B) knickers
    C) knotted
    D) knowledge

13. LACKADAISICAL
    A) lacquer
    B) lanky
    C) larder
    D) latitude

14. HOTHEADED
    A) homelessness
    B) honesty
    C) horrifying
    D) Houston

15. KIMBERLY
    A) kibble
    B) Kierkegaard
    C) Kipling
    D) kites

16. MARRIED
    A) Marco
    B) Maria
    C) market
    D) marvel

17. COFFEE
    A) cocoa
    B) Cooper
    C) corning
    D) cozier

18. DIVERT
    A) diaphragm
    B) direct
    C) discord
    D) divest

19. TULIP
    A) tuba
    B) Tuckahoe
    C) tufted
    D) turntable

20. LINGER
    A) licorice
    B) lipstick
    C) liquor
    D) lizard

21. PATTER
    A) pacify
    B) papaya
    C) Paris
    D) Pavel

22. RIBBIT
    A) ribald
    B) ribbing
    C) ribcage
    D) ribeye

23. CONSOLIDATION
    A) condor
    B) confidence
    C) conjoined
    D) continent

24. DUBAI
    A) dubbing
    B) dubious
    C) Dublin
    D) dubs

25. ADDRESS
    A) addiction
    B) additional
    C) additive
    D) adductor

DIRECTIONS: Determine where the bolded name should be filed in the group: A if it should be first, B if it should be second, C if it should be third, D if it should be fourth.

26. Stavros Xenos
    David Xiao
    Glenna Xavier
    Xerox Corporation

    A) First
    B) Second
    C) Third
    D) Fourth

27. Sunny Richards
    Leila Richardson
    Joyce Richard
    Rhonda Ricardo

    A) First
    B) Second
    C) Third
    D) Fourth

28. Yolanda Thomson
    Rodney Thompkins
    V. Tomkins
    Wanda Thompson

    A) First
    B) Second
    C) Third
    D) Fourth

29. **American Airlines Corp.**
    James Armstrong
    J. Armey
    Jonathan Armstrong

    A) First
    B) Second
    C) Third
    D) Fourth

30. Lisa Chambers
    Kim Cho
    Alexia Chamberlain
    Delshawn Chalmers

    A) First
    B) Second
    C) Third
    D) Fourth

31. Brandi Nguyen
    Oliver Norris
    Mickey Norhill
    95th Street Block Assn.

    A) First
    B) Second
    C) Third
    D) Fourth

32. T. Velazquez
    Torrey Vickey
    Tanya Vickers
    Thomas Vickers

    A) First
    B) Second
    C) Third
    D) Fourth

33. Mike Mendez
    Ilana McLellan
    Sarah Maloney
    David McNally

    A) First
    B) Second
    C) Third
    D) Fourth

34. Kitty Grimwald
    L. Gordon
    Doug Gordon-Jackson
    Carlos Gosselin

    A) First
    B) Second
    C) Third
    D) Fourth

CONTINUE →

35.

Ryan Oliver
Jordan O'Sullivan
Rodney Orange
Joey Olivares

A) First
B) Second
C) Third
D) Fourth

36.

Jackie Ronaldo
Jermaine Ross
Jerry Rosenstein
J. Ronaldo

A) First
B) Second
C) Third
D) Fourth

37.

L. Green
Han F. Gu
F.L. Greenberg
Courtney F. Gunnerson

A) First
B) Second
C) Third
D) Fourth

38.

Amy Mitchell
Lakshmi R. Malkin
Roger Munoz
The Microsoft Corp.

A) First
B) Second
C) Third
D) Fourth

39.

Tesla, Inc.
Shawn Y. Taylor
The Target Company
T.J. Maxx, Inc.

A) First
B) Second
C) Third
D) Fourth

40.

Larry R. Appleton
Apple, Inc.
Archer Farms, Inc.
Axios Technologies, LLC

A) First
B) Second
C) Third
D) Fourth

DIRECTIONS: Select the name that would be **third** if the group were correctly alphabetized.

41.

A) Kim Gorman
B) K. Gorman
C) Kyle Grimes
D) Karen Galligan

42.

A) Julianna Morales
B) J.P. Morales
C) Julianna P. Morales
D) Julianna Perez Morales

43.

A) Vincent Wu
B) Jerry Wilkins
C) V. Williamson
D) J.R. Watkins

44.

A) Graystar Management, LLC
B) Jamal R. Garrison
C) The Galley Group
D) Tobias Greenwich

45.

    A) Fortis Healthcare Ltd.

    B) Sam Forrest-Waller

    C) Carly R. Foster

    D) Future Retail Ltd.

46.

    A) P.T. Delgado

    B) Delilah de la Vega

    C) Andrea D'Souza

    D) B. Thomas Derringer

47.

    A) Casey Whittaker

    B) Worthington Industries, LLC

    C) Ophelia L. Waxworth

    D) O.L. Whitman

48.

    A) Ellen La Grange

    B) Lois Lefkowitz

    C) Amelia R. Lockwood

    D) D.B. Lagrange

49.

    A) Jasmine Granby

    B) Doris Gorsky

    C) The Glickman Photography Co.

    D) J.B. Gorsky

50.

    A) Ahmed El Hajj

    B) Wilson E. Elkins

    C) R.V. Elkinson

    D) Victoria Engels

51.

    A) Jennifer N. Hill

    B) Mike Hernandez

    C) Van Hidalgo

    D) Portia Hernandez

52.

    A) Lawrence N. Colbert

    B) Lawrence Colbert

    C) R.N. Colbert

    D) Quentin T. Colbert

53.

    A) Thayer E. Heisenberg

    B) T.L. Heisenweiss

    C) Hess Petroleum Co.

    D) Tyrone E. Hellman

54.

    A) Julian R. Burrows

    B) Julian Burrows

    C) William R. Burroughs

    D) Kiana S. Burroughs

55.

    A) Richard Jackson Longview

    B) Richard J. Longview

    C) Juliana P. Longview

    D) Giuliana Longview

Filing Names

DIRECTIONS: Choose the space where the given name should be filled.

1. Bryant, Alexander B.

    A) −Bayan, Eduardo M.

    B) −Bryan, Alison

    C) −Bryant, Alyssa

    D) −Byers, Warren E.

    E)

2. Worthington, Jillian L.

    A) −Wellington, Ariana

    B) −Wimberly, Claudia

    C) −Worthington, Alexander P.

    D) −Worthington, Jonathan

    E) −

3. Lee, Daniel
   A) –Le, Wilbur M.
   B) –Lee, Derek
   C) –Leigh, Lewis
   D) –Li, William
   E) –

4. Rodriguez, Jennifer
   A) –Ramirez, Arthur P.
   B) –Rodrigo, Tony M.
   C) –Rodrigues, Wally
   D) –Rodriguez, Whitney
   E) –

5. Watkins, Jimmy
   A) –Wadd, Grover L.
   B) –Watkins, Monica
   C) –Watson, Ophelia
   D) –Watsons, Victoria
   E) –

6. Wan, Charles
   A) –Wan, Rodney
   B) –Wang, Van
   C) –Wing, Vinh
   D) –Wu, Alex
   E) –

7. Appelbaum, Margaret
   A) –Appelbaum, Matthew
   B) –Appelberg, Winston
   C) –Applebright, Alexander
   D) –Appleton, Katherine
   E) –

8. Jenkins, Rosie
   A) –Jankins, Aubrey
   B) –Jenkins, Goldie
   C) –Jenks, Nathaniel
   D) –Junkins, Polly
   E) –

9. Jackson, Ahmed
   A) –Jackman, Andy
   B) –Jackson, Brian
   C) –Jansen, Bryan
   D) –Jenson, Dolly
   E) –

10. Shapiro, Mary Beth
    A) –Schapiro, Gordon
    B) –Schipper, Mary
    C) –Shapiro, Abagail
    D) –Spiro, Joan R.
    E) –

11. McEnaney, Lachlan
    A) –McEarney, Oscar
    B) –McEnaney, Elliot
    C) –McKinley, Andrea
    D) –McKinney, Sean
    E) –

12. Haji, Muhammad
    A) –Haji, Fatima
    B) –Hajime, Omar
    C) –Hajji, Linda
    D) –Hajji, Marwan
    E) –

13. Ivanov, Eugene
    A) –Ivan, Elihu
    B) –Ivanhoe, Arnold M.
    C) –Ivanov, Evgeni
    D) –Ivanovich, Ariana
    E) –

14. Goldstein, Judith P.
    A) –Goldberg, James L.
    B) –Golden, Veronica
    C) –Goldenstein, Moshe R.
    D) –Goldstein, Edward
    E) –

15. Hill, Tiana
  A) –Hall, Kevin R.
  B) –Halls, Winfred R.
  C) –Hill, Roland
  D) –Hills, Albert
  E) –

16. Martin, Wilma S.
  A) –Martin, Holly Y.
  B) –Martinez, Juan L.
  C) –Martino, Nevaeh
  D) –Martins, Iris O.
  E) –

17. Carter, Michael C.
  A) –Cabell, Barry
  B) –Campbell, Zion B.
  C) –Carder, Seth
  D) –Carter, Hilda E.
  E) –

18. Mitchell, Josiah
  A) –Michell, Jeremy
  B) –Michells, Glenda
  C) –Mitchell, Aramecia
  D) –Mitchells, Anna
  E) –

19. Wright, Sarah
  A) –Wraight, Yaela
  B) –Wrate, Alan
  C) –Wright, Susanna
  D) –Wrightson, Donald
  E) –

20. Ackerman, Bryan
  A) –Ackerman, Elijah
  B) –Ackermann, Flora
  C) –Akerman, Sheila S.
  D) –Akermann, Quentin T.
  E) –

21. Weismann, Hershel
  A) –Weismann, Stephen S.
  B) –Weitzman, Abraham
  C) –Weitzmann, Bernard L.
  D) –Weizmann, John
  E) –

22. Taylor, Matilda
  A) – Tailor, Kiara
  B) – Tayler, Ethan
  C) – Taylor, Destiny
  D) – Tyler, Joshua
  E) –

23. Fullerman, Tiffany
  A) –Fuelleman, Alison
  B) –Fuellemann, Mathias
  C) –Fulleman, Bertha
  D) –Fullerman, Jordan
  E) –

24. Lopez, Jasmine
  A) –Lapis, Ethan
  B) –Lapiz, Gabriella R.
  C) –Lopes, Ariana P.
  D) –Lopez, Jesus E.
  E) –

25. Moore, Malik
  A) –Moore, Hailey
  B) –Moore, Justin
  C) –Morris, Joan T.
  D) –Morrison, Thayer
  E) –

Communication and Judgment

DIRECTIONS: Read about each situation and choose the best resolution.

> **EXAMPLE:** An administrative assistant notices her coworker removes office supplies without accounting for them in the log. She believes the coworker is taking them home for personal use. The correct first action to take is
>
> **A)** confront the coworker and accuse him of theft and illegal personal use of government property.
>
> **B)** report the coworker to the supervisor for improper use of office supplies and theft of government property.
>
> **C)** ask the coworker what is happening to the missing office supplies and remind him to note them in the log.
>
> **D)** ignore the situation and hope it goes away because it is none of her business.

> **C)** The administrative assistant should start by asking her coworker about the missing supplies and reminding him to use the log. It is possible that her coworker is using the supplies honestly, and he simply forgot to note in the log the supplies he used to restock his desk or to complete at-home work that his supervisor has asked him to do remotely. If the situation continues, then the administrative assistant should involve the supervisor.

1. A county board of supervisors has declared an 8 p.m. curfew due to a recent series of peaceful protest marches that have degenerated into looting after dark. In a nonemergency call, a citizen phones her local police precinct and asks if she and her husband may walk their dog in their neighborhood after 8 p.m. What should the officer answering the citizen's phone call tell the citizen?

   A) If the citizen sounds like an older person who probably wouldn't break the law, the officer should give her and her husband permission to disregard the curfew.

   B) The officer should ask the caller if she plans to do any looting that night. If the citizen promises not to do any looting, the officer should allow the citizen and her husband to walk their dog after 8 p.m.

   C) The officer should courteously inform the citizen that she and her husband should complete their dog walk before 8 p.m. as long the curfew remains in effect.

   D) The officer should sternly order the citizen to obey the curfew. The officer should remind the citizen that owning a dog does not give her special privileges.

2. An administrative assistant's supervisor asks her out on a date. She politely but firmly refuses, but the supervisor continues to ask again every few weeks. The correct first action to take is

   A) ask for help from the organization's human resources department.

   B) warn the other women in the office to beware of the supervisor.

   C) confront the supervisor and accuse him of sexual harassment.

   D) find out who the supervisor's boss is, and immediately tell that person.

3. A clerical worker's coworker asks if the clerical worker will substitute for him when he goes on vacation the following month. The clerical worker should

   A) agree to do so if she can, but make sure their supervisor knows about the plan.

   B) inform her coworker that she cannot possibly do her own job and his as well.

   C) go to the supervisor and inform her that the coworker has broken the rules concerning vacation time.

   D) find someone else in the office who is willing to substitute for their coworker.

4. A government inspector is doing a routine inspection and notices four different potential problems in a building's basement. Which of these is an emergency that needs immediate attention?

   A) Some children seem to be playing hide-and-seek in the basement.

   B) There is a smell of marijuana smoke lingering in the basement.

   C) There is a leak in a gas pipe.

   D) There is a leak in a sewer pipe.

5. Two clerical workers have noticed that a coworker habitually fails to do his share of a workload that the three of them share. The correct first action to take is

   A) confront the coworker and accuse him of being lazy and selfish.

   B) report the coworker to the supervisor in hopes that he will be replaced with someone who does their share.

   C) explain the situation to the coworker and ask whether there is anything the two can do to help him get up to speed.

   D) ignore the situation and hope it goes away because they are not their coworker's bosses and do not want their coworker to think badly of them.

6. During a statewide epidemic, a toll collector tries to protect herself and the public from infection by wearing a homemade cloth mask and using hand sanitizer. However, many of the drivers she deals with do not seem to be taking similar precautions. Which is the most appropriate response?

   A) She should immediately quit her job and begin collecting unemployment payments.

   B) She should stop worrying—probably she will not contract the illness.

   C) She should refuse to deal with drivers who are not following the county health department's rules.

   D) She should ask her supervisor to provide the best protective gear available.

7. Under which circumstances may a police officer stop a driver, ask him or her to get out of the car, search the driver, and then search the vehicle?

   A) The driver failed to stop fully at a stop sign; also, the officer has a "hunch" that the driver is a criminal.

   B) The driver was driving 10 miles per hour over the speed limit; other than that, he seems like an ordinary citizen who didn't mean to break the law.

   C) The driver was driving erratically and failed to stop fully at a stop sign; after the officer pulls him over and the driver rolls down the window, the officer smells alcohol on the driver's breath.

   D) The driver was driving 15 miles per hour over the speed limit; after the officer pulls him over, the officer notices that the car is filled with a jumble of clothing, sports equipment, and used fast-food containers.

8. A mail carrier occasionally notices a problem that prompts her to ask for help from another city department. Which of these situations constitutes an emergency that she should report right away?

   A) A dog barks and growls loudly at her from inside a home's closed screen door.

   B) She hears a man inside a home yelling at a scared-sounding woman and then hears a loud crash that seems to indicate a physical fight.

   C) She notices that one of families to whom she delivers mail habitually leaves their sprinklers on even though there is a severe drought in the region.

   D) A woman to whom she delivers mail might be living alone and seems to have Alzheimer's disease or another form of dementia.

9. An administrative assistant's supervisor seems to have a grudge against him. The supervisor often criticizes the assistant's work and never gives positive feedback when the assistant completes assignments thoroughly and quickly. The correct first action to take is

   A) compare notes with coworkers who have the same supervisor. If they have had similar experiences with the person, perhaps the supervisor is simply a strict person who treats everyone alike.

   B) ask for an appointment with the head of the organization and complain to them about the supervisor's unkind treatment.

   C) confront the supervisor and accuse her of unfair treatment; threaten to quit if things don't improve.

   D) ask for an appointment with the supervisor; politely ask if she can provide a list of ways the assistant's work can improve. The assistant should make it clear that he wants to do the best he can.

10. While you are completing a routine clerical assignment that is not time sensitive, a coworker asks if you can help him complete a different assignment that has top priority. The correct action to take is

    A) help your coworker complete the top-priority assignment. Then go back to your own assignment and complete it.

    B) report your coworker to the supervisor for being lazy and taking you away from your assigned duties.

    C) tell your coworker to ask someone else for help who is not as busy as you are right now.

    D) complete your own assignment first. Then work with your coworker to complete the top-priority project.

11. A police officer on patrol at 4 a.m. notices smoke coming from the top floor of an apartment building. The correct first action to take is to

    A) find out whether there is actually a fire in the building.

    B) enter the building and warn all the tenants to evacuate.

    C) call the dispatch operator and inform her that he, the officer, is dealing with an emergency.

    D) call the fire department immediately.

12. A supervisor has a clerical assistant who consistently makes errors that cause extra work for the supervisor—she always has to double-check the assistant's work and often needs to redo it. The correct first action to take is

    A) confront the assistant and accuse him of laziness. Maybe he will improve.

    B) transfer the assistant to another department without telling him why.

    C) meet with the assistant and talk over the situation with him. Provide more training if necessary. The supervisor should clearly explain the problems and state her expectations for improvement.

    D) ignore the situation and hope it will get better because she likes the assistant personally—it's his work habits that cause a problem, and she doesn't really mind the extra work.

13. A clerical worker repeatedly complains to the custodian that his workspace is poorly lit. The custodian should

    A) ignore the clerical worker because he is a chronic complainer who will never be satisfied.

    B) investigate the situation to see if it can be remedied by cleaning light fixtures or installing brighter bulbs.

    C) call a licensed electrician and hire him to replace all the lighting in the room where the clerical worker's workspace is located.

    D) ask the boss if the clerical worker has a right to ask for special favors, such as state-of-the-art lighting.

14. In a government office, personal items like purses, wallets, watches, jewelry, and cell phones begin to go missing. Most of the workers suspect a new member of the cleaning crew. The office supervisor should

    A) speak to the head of the cleaning crew and find out if the new cleaner has been properly vetted; if not, the supervisor should ask the crew head to fire the suspect.

    B) make a detailed police report and then ask a security guard to conduct a surprise search of the cleaning crew members' lockers, satchels, and cars.

    C) provide a lockable desk drawer or locker for each worker and tell them to leave their valuables at home or keep them locked up at all times.

    D) do nothing unless or until someone actually witnesses the thief in the act of stealing items.

15. Your boss has hired a new employee who is very intelligent but does not have great social skills. Over time, it becomes clear that some of his behaviors are not appropriate in the workplace; working with this person is very challenging. Which of these behaviors might justify you and your coworkers in signing a petition that asks your boss to terminate the young man's employment?

    A) The young man is very quiet. He rarely speaks when coworkers are chatting in the lunchroom, and he never laughs when someone makes a joke.

    B) The young man flies into rages when he feels threatened. This occurs fairly often. He shouts and slams his cell phone against his desk.

    C) Gifted at computer skills himself, the young man occasionally grows impatient with coworkers when they do not understand his explanations of technical processes.

    D) The young man is socially awkward. He occasionally makes blunt remarks about coworkers' lunches smelling strongly of garlic or other strong odors.

16. Imagine that you are a clerical worker. Your supervisor is not adept at typing or other computer skills, so he writes documents by hand, in pen or pencil, and asks his assistant to input the information for him. Then he asks you to proofread each document by comparing his handwritten manuscript to the printed-out copy. You find this task very tedious. Which is the best solution?

    A) Complete the task cheerfully and well. Clerical workers need to pay close attention to details. Possibly you are not well suited for this kind of work.

    B) Try to find someone else in the office who enjoys proofreading. Give the task to them to complete.

    C) Politely decline to do this task. Your boss should be proofreading his own documents, especially since he refuses to develop better computer skills.

    D) Make an appointment with someone in your organization's human resources department. It is their job to mediate between you and your boss in situations like this one.

17. Often, corrections officers are responsible for deciding whether to handcuff inmates. A corrections officer is legally responsible for using handcuffing to keep inmates and others safe. In which situation is a corrections officer most likely to need to handcuff an inmate?

    A) Claiming to be sick, an inmate refuses to leave his cell for meals.

    B) Out of control, an inmate repeatedly pounds his fists against the bars of his cell.

    C) An inmate repeatedly starts shouting matches with other inmates during mealtimes.

    D) An inmate is keeping other inmates awake at night by reading aloud and singing.

18. An administrative assistant sometimes eats lunch with two of her coworkers, with whom she enjoys spending time. One day she overhears the two of them making plans to spend time together after work, but they do not invite her to join them. What should she do?

    A) Confront the two coworkers and accuse them of hurting her feelings.

    B) Report the two coworkers to the supervisor for treating her, the assistant, disrespectfully.

    C) Ask the coworker whom she likes best to have lunch with her (without inviting the other coworker).

    D) Let it go. As in the wider world, no one in a workplace is obligated to make friends with anyone else.

19. When might a parking agent need to immediately call another city department for help?

   A) He notices two teenage girls whom he suspects of shoplifting nail polish in a pharmacy.

   B) He sees a downed electrical wire that is sparking near pedestrians on a sidewalk.

   C) He gets into an argument with someone who is angry because she has received a parking ticket.

   D) He realizes that the city's street sweepers have not cleaned a certain block in many months.

20. A police officer is stationed on a main city street while a parade passes by. The officer's supervisor has told her not to let any cars cross the street during the parade. However, an EMT driver carrying a gravely ill patient to a nearby hospital pulls up next to the officer and asks if he may cross the parade route. The correct first action to take is to

   A) phone headquarters and ask to speak to the supervisor. It is best to obtain permission even though this is an emergency situation.

   B) report the EMT driver to his supervisor for attempting to cross the street, possibly injuring parade marchers.

   C) quickly stop the parade marchers and allow the EMT driver to cross the parade route, since the patient's life is at stake.

   D) use mapping software to help the EMT driver find a route to the hospital that does not cross the parade route, even though the new route will add 15 minutes to the trip.

Comparison Questions

Directions: Read the names or numbers. Compare and decide how they relate. Mark accordingly on your answer sheet:

   A) if ALL FOUR names or numbers are exactly ALIKE

   B) if TWO of the names or numbers are exactly ALIKE

   C) if THREE names or numbers are exactly ALIKE

   D) if ALL FOUR names or numbers are DIFFERENT

1. Holly McElmurry   Hollie McElmurry
    Holly MacElmurry   Hollie McMurry

2. 2145 Basil Ln.   2145 Basel Ln.
    2145 Basil Ln.   2145 Basil Lane

3. Dan Pine   Daniel Pine
    D.B. Pine   Daniel B. Pine

4. 921 Key Route   921 Key Route
    921 Key Route   921 Key Route

5. Robin Richmond   Robyn Richmond
    Robin Richmond   Robin Richmond

6. 30 E. Columbia St. 30 E. Columbia St.
    30 E. Columbia St. 30 E. Columbia St.

7. Joel Jacobsen   Joel Jacobson
    Joelle Jacobsen   Joel R. Jacobsen

8. Albany, CA 94706   Albany, NY 94706
    Albany, CA 94706   Albany, CA 94707

9. Andrew Kirsh   Andrew Kirsh
    Andrew L. Kirsh   Andrew Kirsch

10. 77 Domingo   771 Domingo
    77 Domingo Ave.   77 Domingo Avenue

11. Audrey Quiet   Audrey Quiet
    Aubrey Quiet   Audrey Quiet

12. 830 Race St.   830 Race St.
    830 Race Street   830 Race St.

13. Alexa A. Orosz   Alexa A. Orosz
    Alexa A. Orosz   Alexa A. Orosz

14. Denver, CO 80123   Denver, Colo. 80123
    Denver, CO 80122   Denver, CO 80123

15. Virginia Faxon   Virginia Faxon
    Virginia Faxen   Virginia Faxon

DIRECTIONS: Compare the sets of names and codes in each question and look for mistakes. The names and codes on the same line should be identical. Mark accordingly on your answer sheet:

- **A)** if ALL THREE of the sets have mistakes
- **B)** if TWO of the sets have mistakes
- **C)** if ONE of the sets has a mistake
- **D)** if there are NO MISTAKES in any of the sets

16. Stephen G. White N7982
Steven G. White N7982

Shawn Whitehorse R1126
Shawn Whitehouse R1126

Michael Solomon Q1369
Michael Salomon Q1369

17. Robin M. Borok J9291
Robin M. Borok J9291

Michael G. Borok J9292
Michele G. Borok J9292

Michelle Chitayat A1012
Michelle Chitayat A1012

18. Julia M. Dorn F4756
Julia M. Dorn F4756

Carrie Seaman V9843
Carrie Seaman V9843

Marjorie Holabird Q5675
Marjorie Holman Q5675

19. Derek Peterson E9167
Derek Petersen E9167

Meredyth Carrick R0526
Meredith Carrick R0526

Alexandra M. Behr W4557
Alexandra M. Behr W5457

20. Robert J. Fresco B1971
Robert J. Fresco B1971

Anthony Morel T1998
Anthony Morell T1998

Michael S. Goldman S2020
Michael S. Goldman S2002

21. Randy Mellon M4464
Randy Mellon M4454

Marc Rushford R9883
Mark Rushford R9883

Oliver Lampton K5554
Oliver Lampkin K5554

22. Lara W. Inglis J9535
Lara W. Inglis J9535

Grace LaBlonde L1875
Grace LaBlonde L1875

Caroline M. Quiner S1855
Caroline M. Quiner S1855

23. Lionel Zimmer B2143
Lionel Zimmer B2143

Elizabeth Zither P2147
Elizabeth Zipher P2147

Betty Lee Mansion X7755
Betty Lee Manshin X7755

24. Linda Twomey P1965
Linda Twomey P1965

Jack Toomey R1999
Jack Toomey R1999

Velma Beverley T1115
Velma Beverley T1115

25. Ken R. Nicolas B2221
Ken R. Nicolas B2221

Kenneth Ellyson L1992
Kenneth Ellison L1992

David G. Clark I1978
David G. Clark J1978

26. Diana Chirac I2015
Diane Chirac I2015

Aaron L. Pine C1975
Aaron L. Pine C1965

Lucas O. Pine M2019
Lucas P. Pine M2019

27. Peggy Strawberry J1954
Peggy Strawberry J1954

Patrick Stinson N1444
Patrick Stinson N1444

Peter Brixton S4557
Peter Brixton S4557

28. Lana R. Ryder F1642
Lana R. Ryder F1642

Grant Mannering F1555
Grant Mannering F1555

Pamela T. Huntsman H1492
Pamela T. Huntsman H1492

29. Ursula Stepson B7763
Ursula Stepsen B7763

Cindy E. Heron F1401
Cindy E. Herron F1401

Valerie Godmersham M1357
Valerie Godmersham M1357

30. Daniel R. Lester A1955
Daniel B. Lester A1955

Robert Harrington K1957
Robert Herrington K1957

Leo T. Pynewood S1921
Leo T. Pynewood S1922

Coding Questions

DIRECTIONS: Each letter should be matched with its number as in the table below.

LETTER	Q	W	E	R	T	Y	U	P	S
NUMBER	9	8	7	6	5	4	3	2	1

Read the letters and numbers to determine if they match according to the table. Mark accordingly on your answer sheet:

A) if ALL THREE sets are correct.

B) if TWO of the sets are matched correctly.

C) if ONE of the sets is matched correctly.

D) if NONE of the sets is matched correctly.

1. PQTY 2954
STWE 1587
RQPU 6923

2. PUST 2415
WEQS 8891
SEWT 1795

3. WERT 1954
SPUR 1972
QTUP 2121

4. YUPQ 4329
PUTW 2358
TUPE 6327

5. REWS 1865
PSTR 1786
QWER 9876

6. REST 2461
TYUP 5432
SQWE 1234

7. STUE 1437
WEPS 4326
EQRS 7961

8. YUPW 8753
REWP 6782
SPUR 1236

9. RUPS 6321
SWET 1875
QRST 9615

10. RRUP 6632
QWER 9872
TYUP 5439

DIRECTIONS: Each letter should be matched with its number as in the table below.

LETTER	A	S	D	F	G	H	J	K	L
NUMBER	0	1	2	3	4	5	6	7	8

Read the letters and numbers to determine if they match according to the table. Mark accordingly on your answer sheet:

A) if ALL THREE sets are correct.

B) if TWO of the sets are matched correctly.

C) if ONE of the sets is matched correctly.

D) if NONE of the sets is matched correctly.

11. DAFL 2038
     FAKS 8070
     KLDF 7823

12. SHAD 1502
     ADFG 0864
     KLGH 8625

13. ASDF 0123
     GHJK 4567
     LASD 8012

14. FLAK 3807
     DAGK 2047
     SKLK 1787

15. FADS 3051
     LADS 8025
     JADS 6047

16. ASDF 0156
     FDSA 3247
     HJKL 5601

17. GGKK 4477
     DDFF 2233
     LLAA 8800

18. SKAH 1705
     SLAK 1807
     GLAS 1865

19. DFKL 1802
     ASKL 1765
     FGAS 3401

20. FLAG 3804
     GLAS 1491
     DAHS 2017

→

CONTINUE

Memorization

DIRECTIONS: Take TWO minutes to review the image below. Then answer the questions without looking at the image.

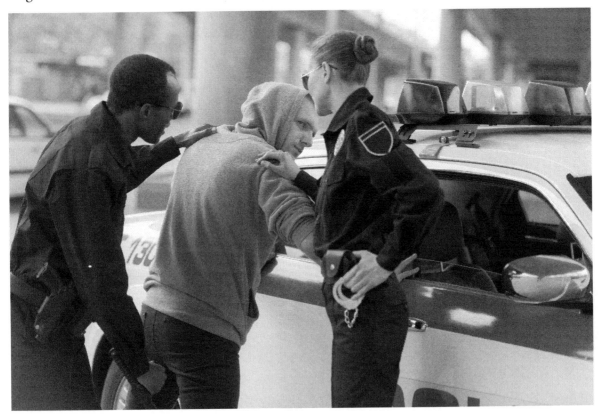

1. What is the suspect in the photograph wearing?

   A) a costume

   B) jeans and a hooded sweatshirt

   C) a jumpsuit

   D) shorts and T-shirt

2. What is the subject leaning against in the photograph?

   A) a wall

   B) a pillar

   C) a fence

   D) a squad car

3. What is the female police officer gripping with her left hand in the photograph?

   A) the suspect

   B) the other police officer's shoulder

   C) handcuffs

   D) the squad car

DIRECTIONS: Take TWO minutes to review the image below. Then answer the questions without looking at the image.

4. What is pictured in the upper-left-hand corner of the photograph?

   A) a hubcap

   B) broken glass

   C) caution tape

   D) a person on the ground

5. What number is the officer placing near the crime scene?

   A) 1

   B) 2

   C) 3

   D) 4

6. How many people are pictured in the photograph?

   A) one

   B) two

   C) three

   D) four

CONTINUE

Directions: Take TWO minutes to review the image below. Then answer the questions without looking at the image.

7. What is the person in the photograph gripping in their right hand?

    A) a gun
    B) a magnifying glass
    C) a brush
    D) a cell phone

8. How many markers are visible on the ground in the photograph?

    A) one
    B) two
    C) three
    D) four

9. What is the presumed location of the crime scene?

    A) a paved city parking lot
    B) a police station
    C) a wooded area
    D) a playground

DIRECTIONS: Take TWO minutes to review the image below. Then answer the questions without looking at the image.

10. What is the police officer on the left MOST LIKELY doing in the photograph?

    A) questioning a suspect

    B) frisking a suspect

    C) detaining a suspect

    D) directing traffic

11. What is the suspect in the photograph kneeling next to?

    A) a squad car

    B) another suspect

    C) a traffic cone

    D) a fence

12. Which way is the suspect's head facing in the photograph?

    A) to the right

    B) to the left

    C) away from the camera

    D) toward the camera

CONTINUE ⟶

DIRECTIONS: Take TWO minutes to review the image below. Then answer the questions without looking at the image.

13. What does it say on the officer's vest in the photograph?

   A) EVENTS

   B) POLICE

   C) LAPD

   D) NYPD

14. Which direction is the closest car driving in the photograph?

   A) from right to left

   B) from left to right

   C) toward the camera

   D) away from the camera

15. What is the police officer MOST LIKELY doing in the photograph?

   A) detaining a suspect

   B) patrolling in a squad car

   C) directing traffic and pedestrian crossings

   D) securing a crime scene

ANSWER KEY

READING

1. **B)** The author writes that because hand sanitizer "isn't rinsed from hands [as is water], it only kills pathogens and does nothing to remove organic matter."

2. **D)** The author writes that "hands 'cleaned' with hand sanitizer may still harbor pathogens" because sanitizer "does nothing to remove organic matter" from the hands. The bacteria are not completely washed off, and therefore some are able to continue living on the surface of the hands.

3. **B)** In the second paragraph, the author writes, "The [hand washing] process doesn't even require warm water—studies have shown that cold water is just as effective at reducing the number of microbes on the hands. Antibacterial soaps are also available, although several studies have shown that simple soap and cold water are just as effective."

4. **C)** Together, these sentences provide an adequate summary of the passage overall.

5. **A)** Each paragraph examines hand washing from a different angle.

6. **A)** In the first paragraph, the author writes, "Many illnesses are spread when people touch infected surfaces, such as door handles or other people's hands, and then touch their own eyes, mouths, or noses." The reader can infer

from this sentence that hand washing prevents the spread of surface-borne illnesses.

7. **B)** The author writes that "as these communities have evolved, the species in them have developed complex, long-term interspecies interactions known as symbiotic relationships." She then goes on to describe the different types of symbiotic relationships that exist.

8. **D)** The author writes, "Often, relationships described as commensal include one species that feeds on another species' leftovers; remoras, for instance, will attach themselves to sharks and eat the food particles they leave behind. It might seem like the shark gets nothing from the relationship, but a closer look will show that sharks in fact benefit from remoras, which clean the sharks' skin and remove parasites."

9. **C)** The author writes, "A relationship where one individual benefits and the other is harmed is known as parasitism."

10. **A)** The author writes that "there's another class of symbiosis that is controversial among scientists" and goes on to say that "many scientists claim the relationships currently described as commensal are just mutualistic or parasitic in ways that haven't been discovered

yet." This implies that scientists debate about the topic of commensalism.

11. **A)** The author writes, "But is it possible for two species to interact and for one to remain completely unaffected?... In fact, many scientists claim that relationships currently described as commensal are just mutualistic or parasitic in ways that haven't been discovered yet."

12. **D)** The author writes, "The bacteria, fungi, insects, plants, and animals that live together in a habitat have evolved to share a pool of limited resources. As these communities have evolved, the species in them have developed complex, long-term interspecies interactions known as symbiotic relationships."

13. **A)** This choice addresses all of the main ideas of the passage: the flu is potentially deadly, highly infectious, and difficult to contain due to viral shedding.

14. **D)** According to the passage, "the flu is... relatively difficult to contract," and "while many people who contract the virus will recover, many others will not."

15. **C)** The second paragraph states that the flu is "relatively difficult to contract" because it "can only be transmitted when individuals come into direct contact with bodily fluids of people infected with the flu or when they are exposed to expelled aerosol particles."

16. **A)** The author uses the term *measures* to describe the steps that people to take to prevent the spreading of the influenza virus.

17. **C)** The final paragraph of the passage states that viral shedding is "the process by which the body releases viruses that have been successfully reproducing during the infection."

18. **A)** The second paragraph of the passage states that "the virus can be contained with fairly simple health measures like hand washing and face masks."

19. **C)** The first sentence in the second paragraph states the paragraph's main idea: "Men are more likely to exhibit riskier behaviors than women, especially between the ages of fifteen and twenty-four, when testosterone production is at its peak."

20. **B)** The primary purpose of the essay is to explain or give reasons; its focus is the gender gap in life expectancy, as the title shows. It is not advisory or cautionary, and it does not express the author's hopes.

21. **D)** In the first paragraph, the author writes, "Across the globe, women are, on average, outliving their male counterparts. Although this gender gap has shrunk over the last decade, … women are still expected to live four and a half years longer than men." The passage does not support any of the other statements.

22. **C)** In the second paragraph, the author implies that young women do not behave as riskily as young men do. In the fourth paragraph, the author states that men "may be less likely to eat as many fruits and vegetables as their female counterparts. And [men] may be more likely to consume more red meat, including processed meat. These types of meats have been linked to high cholesterol, hypertension, and cancer." In general, the author describes women as more sensible than men when it comes to physical safety and a healthy lifestyle.

23. **C)** In the first paragraph, the author writes that the "gender gap has shrunk over the last decade thanks to medical improvements and lifestyle changes." Readers can infer from this that the average man has a healthier lifestyle than he did over ten years ago.

24. **A)** In the third paragraph, the author writes, "Estrogen…seems to be correlated with cholesterol levels: an increase in estrogen is accompanied by a decrease in 'bad' cholesterol." Readers can infer that *correlated* means "linked or associated."

25. **C)** The passage is mainly about ways that the overuse of antibiotics has led drug-resistant bacteria to evolve. The other sentences give details from the passage.

26. **D)** In the first sentence, the author writes, "The discovery of penicillin by Alexander Fleming in 1928 revolutionized medical care. The widespread use of penicillin and other antibiotics has saved millions of people from the deadliest bacterial infections known to humans and prevented the spread of bacterial diseases." The context shows that the author uses the word *revolutionized* to refer to an

important discovery that modernized medicine and saved many lives.

27. **D)** The passage does not contain this detail. The passage does not mention other types of farms besides factory farms.

28. **A)** While the author does not explicitly suggest a solution, he or she points out a serious problem that is caused by using antibiotics in harmful ways.

29. **B)** Phrases such as "undermined their effectiveness," "inundating [livestock] with cocktails of antibiotics," "dramatic rise in drug-resistant infections," and "sickening two million people per year and killing 23,000 in the United States alone" show that the author feels very concerned about the problem described in the passage.

30. **D)** In the last two sentences, the author writes, "Because livestock manure is used as fertilizer, drug-resistant bacteria are spreading within the soils and waterways of farms, contaminating even plant-producing environments. The result: a dramatic rise in drug-resistant bacterial infections, sickening two million people per year and killing 23,000 in the United States alone." Readers can infer that by "a dramatic rise," the author means "a very noticeable or striking rise."

VERBAL ABILITY

1. **B)** *Vital* means "related to life; essential to existence or well-being."

2. **A)** *Adhere* means "to follow devotedly; to hold closely to an idea or course."

3. **B)** *Deleterious* means "harmful or deadly to living things."

4. **B)** *Prone* means "lying flat."

5. **D)** *Ambulatory* means "able to walk."

6. **A)** *Superficial* means "shallow in character or attitude; on the surface."

7. **C)** *Malaise* means "a general feeling of illness and discomfort."

8. **A)** *Respiration* means "breathing."

9. **D)** *Transient* means "lasting for only a short period of time."

10. **C)** *Incompatible* means "unable to work together" or "mismatched.""

11. **C)** To *transmit* something is to send it or pass it on.

12. **C)** *Void* can be a noun or a verb, meaning "emptiness" or "to empty or evacuate."

13. **A)** *Therapeutic* means "having a beneficial or healing effect."

14. **A)** *Discreet* means "considerate" or "careful to avoid causing offense or injury."

15. **C)** *Abstain* means "to refrain; choose to avoid or not participate."

16. **B)** Choice B correctly connects two independent clauses ("Kiana went to class" and "Lara stayed home") with a comma and the coordinating conjunction *but*. Choice A incorrectly uses a semicolon instead of a comma. Choice C is a comma splice, using a comma without a coordinating conjunction. Choice D is a run-on sentence, since it lacks a comma before the coordinating conjunction *but*.

17. **C)** Choice C contains the correctly paired conjunctions *either...or*. In choice A, *either* is incorrectly paired with *nor*. Choice B includes a double negative (*can't…neither*), and choice D contains a verb error (*can taking*).

18. **B)** In choice B, the singular proper noun *Pablo* correctly agrees with the singular pronoun *he*. Choices A and C both incorrectly use the adjective *good* instead of the adverb *well*. Choice D incorrectly uses the adjective *diligent* instead of the adverb *diligently*.

19. **D)** Choice D correctly pairs the singular subject *no one* with the singular verb *wants*. Choice A incorrectly pairs the singular subject *one* with the plural verb *hope*. Choice B incorrectly pairs the plural subject *two* with the singular verb *hopes*. Choice C incorrectly pairs the plural subject *all* with the singular verb *hopes*.

20. **D)** Choice D correctly uses the three homophones *they're* (a contraction meaning "they are"), *there* (a noun meaning "that place"), and *their* (a plural possessive pronoun). In choice A, *they're* is incorrectly used instead of *there*. Choice B incorrectly transposes *their* and *there*, and choice C incorrectly uses *their* in place of *they're* or *they are*.

21. **A)** Answers B and C contain a misplaced modifier: *in bags*. It is unclear whether the lunches or the deputies were in bags. Answer C is wordy and changes the meaning of the sentence. Choice D completely changes the meaning of the sentence.

22. **B)** Choice B correctly capitalizes the proper nouns *British Columbia, Canada*; it also correctly lowercases the common nouns *aunt*, *mom's*, and *husband*. In choice A, the common nouns *mom's*, and *husband* are incorrectly capitalized. Choice C incorrectly lowercases *Columbia* (in the proper noun *British Columbia*) and incorrectly capitalizes the common noun *aunt*. Choice D incorrectly capitalizes the common nouns *aunt*, *mom's*, and *husband*.

23. **A)** Choice A correctly compares three people using the suffix *–est*. Choice B incorrectly

compares three people using the suffix –er. Choice C incorrectly uses *most* with a one-syllable adjective, *smart*. Choice D incorrectly uses *more* with a one-syllable adjective, *smart*.

24. **C)** Choice C correctly pairs the compound subject "Brenda and Pauletta" with the plural verb *are*. The adverb *tomorrow* indicates that the deadline is in the future. Therefore, *deadline* cannot take a past-tense verb, making choices A and B incorrect. Choice D is incorrect because the singular verb *is* cannot be paired with the compound subject "Brenda and Pauletta."

25. **C)** Choice C uses the following punctuation marks correctly: an apostrophe in *isn't*, a colon, an apostrophe in *there's*, a comma, another comma, and a period. In choice A, the comma after *home* should be changed to a semicolon or a colon. In choice B, an apostrophe is missing from the contraction *isn't* and from the contraction *there's*. In choice D, the apostrophe in the word *isn't* is misplaced (it is at the end of the word). Also, the question mark after *home* should be changed to a period; the clause "My cat . . . home" forms a statement, not a question.

26. **B)** Choice B correctly pairs the plural noun *parents* with the plural verb *pick* and correctly pairs *either* with *or*. Choice A incorrectly pairs the plural noun *parents* with the singular verb *picks*. Choice C incorrectly pairs *either…nor*, and choice D incorrectly pairs *neither…or*.

27. **A)** Choice A has no misplaced modifiers; this choice makes it clear who burned the soup (Mario) and how he did so (by leaving it on the stove for too long). Choices B and C contain misplaced modifiers that make it seem like Mario was left on the stove for too long. Choice D is incorrectly constructed so that it sounds as if the soup realized that it was burned and Mario was the culprit.

28. **D)** Choice D correctly matches the singular noun *cat* with the singular pronoun *its* and the singular verb *eats*; this choice also correctly matches the plural noun *dogs* with the plural pronoun *their* and the plural verb *sleep*. Choice A incorrectly matches the singular noun *cat* with the plural pronoun *their* and the plural verb *eat*; this choice also incorrectly matches the singular noun *dog* with the plural pronoun *their* and the plural verb *sleep*. Choice B incorrectly matches the plural noun *cats* with the singular possessive pronoun *its* and the

singular verb *eats*; this choice also incorrectly matches the singular noun *dog* with the plural pronoun *their* and the plural verb *sleep*. In choice C, the singular subject *cat* does not match the plural verb *eat* and the plural pronoun *their*.

29. **D)** Choice D correctly capitalizes the proper noun *Microsoft*, leaving the common nouns *automobile* and *industry* in lowercase. Choice A incorrectly capitalizes the common noun *automobile*. In choice B, the proper noun *Microsoft* is incorrectly written in lowercase. Choice C incorrectly capitalizes the common nouns *automobile* and *industry*.

30. **B)** Choice B correctly pairs the plural subject "my teacher and the school principal" with the plural verb *have worked*. Choice A incorrectly pairs the plural subject "my teacher and the school principal" with the singular verb *has worked*. Choice C contains a verb error ("have been worked together"), and choice D also contains a verb error ("had working together").

31. **C)** Choice C uses the following punctuation marks correctly: a colon, a comma, another comma, and a period. In choice A, the parentheses around the name *Jack* are unnecessary, and a colon should follow *order* to indicate a list. In choice B, the semicolon following *order* should be changed to a colon. In choice D, the question mark at the end of the sentence should be changed to a period.

32. **C)** Choice C correctly pairs the singular subject "none of us" with the singular verb *wants*. Choice A incorrectly pairs the singular subject *everyone* with the plural verb *want*. Choice B incorrectly pairs the singular subject *everybody* with the plural verb *want*. Choice D incorrectly pairs the singular subject *nobody* with the plural verb *want*.

33. **A)** Choice A correctly connects two independent clauses, "DeQuan loves eating pizza" and "meat toppings make him feel queasy," using a comma and the coordinating conjunction *but*. Choice B has a misplaced modifier: the dependent clause "though he avoids meat toppings." That clause incorrectly modifies *pizza* when it should modify *DeQuan*. In choice C, the verb *makes* is incorrectly conjugated: it should be plural to match the plural subject *toppings*. Choice D is a run-on sentence; it lacks a comma before *but*.

34. **C)** Choice C correctly capitalizes the proper nouns *Pacific* and *Atlantic*. In choice A, the common noun *oceans* is incorrectly capitalized. Choice B incorrectly capitalizes the common noun *planet* and incorrectly lowercases the proper noun *Pacific*. Choice D incorrectly capitalizes the common nouns *oceans* and *planet* and the adjective *largest*.

35. **C)** Choice C correctly compares two people using the suffix *–er*. Choice A incorrectly uses *most* with a one-syllable adjective, *old*. Choice B incorrectly uses *more* with *older*. Choice D incorrectly compares only two people using the suffix *–est*.

36. **C)** Choice C, *toward*, is correct.

37. **A)** Choice A, *liaison*, is correct.

38. **C)** Choice C, *rescinded*, is correct.

39. **A)** Choice A, *surprised*, is correct.

40. **B)** Choice B, *tendency*, is correct.

41. **A)** Choice A, *necessary*, is correct.

42. **D)** All of the choices are wrong. The word should be spelled *government*.

43. **B)** Choice B, *accommodations*, is correct.

44. **A)** Choice A, *harassing*, is correct.

45. **C)** Choice C, *noticeably*, is correct.

46. **C)** Choice C, *possession*, is correct.

47. **A)** Choice A, *siege*, is correct.

48. **A)** Choice A, *publicly*, is correct.

49. **D)** All of the choices are incorrect. The word should be spelled *aggressive*.

50. **B)** Choice B, *fluorescent*, is correct.

51. **A)** Choice A, *adversarial*, is correct.

52. **C)** Choice C, *germane*, is correct.

53. **B)** Choice B, *palpable*, is correct.

54. **C)** Choice C, *subpoena*, is correct.

55. **B)** Choice B, *suspicious*, is correct.

56. **A)** Comedy and tragedy are antonyms; joy and calamity are antonyms.

57. **B)** Running is fast; walking is slow.

58. **D)** A stop sign and a traffic light are both tools put in place for drivers.

59. **C)** Frantic and desperate are synonyms; angry and irate are synonyms.

60. **B)** A cup and a mug are synonyms; a trophy and a prize are synonyms.

61. **C)** Cookie is a whole; chocolate chips are a part of that whole. Pizza is a whole; pepperoni is a part of that whole.

62. **D)** Recreation and amusement are synonyms; exhaustion and fatigue are synonyms.

63. **B)** A piece is a part of the puzzle; a player is part of a team.

64. **B)** Feathers protect a bird; fur protects a dog.

65. **A)** A tree is part of a forest; a bird is part of a flock.

66. **C)** A train rides on rails; a car rides on roads.

67. **B)** A string is part of a guitar; a lace is part of a shoe.

68. **A)** A lighthouse uses a foghorn; a firetruck uses a siren.

69. **D)** A log is used in a fireplace; a shovel is used in a garden.

70. **B)** A houseplant goes into a flowerpot; brownies go into a pan.

71. **C)** *Subtle* means "delicate or difficult to observe."

72. **C)** *Innocuous* takes its origins from the Latin *in–*, meaning "not," and *nocuus*, meaning

"injurious." Hence, the word means "not injurious or not harmful."

73. **A)** *Amalgam* means "a mixture or blend."

74. **B)** *Adversely* means "harmful to one's interest; unfortunate."

75. **A)** *Potent* means "wielding power; strong; effective."

76. **B)** *Asymmetric* means "lacking symmetry or unbalanced."

77. **C)** *Succumb* means "to yield or stop resisting."

78. **A)** *Excessive* means "exceeding what is normal or necessary."

79. **D)** *Sensible* means having "good sense or reason."

80. **B)** *Justify* means "to show to be just or right."

81. **C)** *Regress* means "to move backward, often to a worse state."

82. **A)** *Pragmatic* means "concerned with practical matters and results."

83. **D)** *Retain* means "to hold or keep in possession." Fluid retention can be a symptom of a medical condition.

84. **D)** *Dysfunctional* means "not functioning properly."

85. **B)** *Diminish* means "become less in amount or intensity."

86. **A)** *Accountability* means "to be responsible for or subject to providing an account."

87. **D)** *Abbreviate* means "to shorten or abridge."

88. **C)** *Cohort* means "a group of people with something in common."

89. **C)** *Benign* means "not harmful; not malignant."

90. **D)** *Consistency* means "conforming to regular patterns, habits, principles," and so on.

91. **A)** Because the second sentence is already so long, it is best not to combine the two.

92. **B)** The singular neuter possessive pronoun *its* agrees with its singular neuter antecedent, *phenomenon*.

93. **C)** Using just one adjective, *novel*, saves the phrase from being redundant.

94. **B)** The plural verb *were* agrees with the plural noun *predecessors*.

95. **A)** The writer used parallel construction, correctly placed phrases, and correct punctuation to write this sentence. It flows smoothly, making it easy to understand.

96. **B)** The adverb *however* makes good sense here. It paves the way for the author to say something negative about push carts that contrasts with their positive qualities.

97. **C)** This clause effectively points out a major difference between the push cart and the modern food truck: a food truck features a full kitchen in miniature, while the push cart did not.

98. **C)** This construction correctly conveys the idea that a chuck wagon was a covered wagon that served as a kitchen.

99. **D)** The sentence provides detailed information on the meaning of *mobile kitchen*.

100. **C)** These trucks were apparently called roach coaches because their grungy kitchens attracted bugs.

101. **B)** This placement fits with the paragraph's chronological order.

102. **A)** The adverbial phrase *in recent years* makes good sense here. It fits in with the phrase *a new trend*, which appears earlier in the passage.

103. **B)** The progressive verb tense in *are flocking* makes good sense here. The author is describing events that are happening in the present day.

104. **D)** This description jives with the first sentence in that they both show people's excitement about the new food trucks.

105. B) As well as giving details about today's food trucks, the essay describes push carts, chuck wagons, roach coaches, and other food-purveying vehicles of the past.

106. B)

107. A)

108. D)

109. A)

110. D)

111. C)

112. D)

113. C)

114. B)

115. B)

MATHEMATICS

1. **D)**

   negative × negative = positive

   $(-9)(-4) =$ **36**

2. **C)**

   $6.3 \div 18 =$ **0.35**

3. **B)**

   $26.5 + 18.9 + 35.1 =$ **80.5**

4. **B)**

   $\frac{1}{2} + \frac{2}{3} + \frac{1}{4}$

   $\frac{6}{12} + \frac{8}{12} + \frac{3}{12} = \frac{17}{12} = \mathbf{1\frac{5}{12}}$

5. **B)**

   $\frac{5}{x} = \frac{7}{14}$

   $7x = 70$

   $\mathbf{x = 10}$

6. **C)**

   part = whole × percent

   $124 \times 0.40 =$ **49.6**

7. **B)**

   $12x + 5 = 77$

   $12x = 72$

   $\mathbf{x = 6}$

8. **B)**

   negative ÷ negative = positive

   $-48 \div (-6) =$ **8**

9. **D)**

   $\$3.49 \times 6 = \$20.94$

   $\$10.49 \times 3 = \$31.47$

   $\$20.94 + \$31.47 = \$52.41$

   $\$100.00 - \$52.41 = \mathbf{\$47.59}$

10. **C)**

    $1.73 + 2.17 =$ **3.9**

11. **B)**

    $3\frac{2}{4} + 3\frac{3}{4} + 4 + 4\frac{1}{4} + 4\frac{2}{4} = 18\frac{8}{4} = 18 + 2 = \mathbf{20}$

12. **A)**

    $\frac{1}{2.5} = \frac{x}{10}$

    $2.5x = 10$

    $\mathbf{x = 4}$

13. **A)**

    whole = $\frac{\text{part}}{\text{percent}}$

    $\frac{26}{0.40} =$ **65**

14. **B)**

    $\$25.44 \div 3.2 =$ **\$7.95**

15. **C)**

    $4 - (-20) = 4 + 20 =$ **24**

16. **C)**

    $9^2 + 2(7^2 - 1) = 81 + 2(49 - 1)$

    $= 81 + 2(48) = 81 + 96 =$ **177**

17. **D)**

    $\$75.00 - \$39.73 =$ **\$35.27**

18. **D)**

    part = whole × percent

    $500 \times 0.70 =$ **350**

19. **D)**

    1 year = 52 weeks

    $1.1 \times 52 = 57.2 \approx$ **57**

20. **C)**

    $\frac{4}{50} = \frac{x}{175}$

    $50x = 700$

    $\mathbf{x = 14}$

21. **B)**

    $\$285.48 \div 6 =$ **\$47.58**

22. **D)**

    $-20 + (-25) =$ **−45**

23. **A)**

    $= (9 + 6) \times (2 - 5) = 15 \times (-3) =$ **−45**

24. A)

$66{,}653.2 - 66{,}284.8 = \mathbf{368.4}$

25. A)

$\$13.50 \times 7.5 = \mathbf{\$101.25}$

26. C)

$\dfrac{2}{7} = \dfrac{72}{x}$

$2x = 504$

$\boldsymbol{x = 252}$

27. B)

$\text{percent} = \dfrac{\text{part}}{\text{whole}}$

$\dfrac{4}{25} = 0.16 = \mathbf{16\%}$

28. D)

$-4x + 2 = -34$

$-4x = -36$

$\boldsymbol{x = 9}$

29. B)

$-2100 + 11{,}200 = \$9100$

$\$9100 \div 2 = \mathbf{\$4550}$

30. B)

$0.8 + 0.49 + 0.89 = 2.18$

$2.5 - 2.18 = \mathbf{0.32}$

CLERICAL SKILLS

Alphabetization

1. B)

Fighters should be filed before *finite*.

2. C)

Victor should be filed before *Vincent*.

3. D)

Prorated should be filed before *protest*.

4. C)

Oblong should be filed before *obnoxious*.

5. A)

Adjacent should be filed before *adjective*.

6. A)

Hydrate should be filed before *hydration*.

7. D)

Whiskers should be filed before *whispers*.

8. B)

Bicycle should be filed before *binoculars*.

9. C)

Gigantic should be filed before *gingerly*.

10. A)

Beach should be filed before *bell*.

11. A)

Excise should be filed before *excite*.

12. C)

Knight should be filed before *knotted*.

13. A)

Lackadaisical should be filed before *lacquer*.

14. D)

Hotheaded should be filed before *Houston*.

15. C)

Kimberly should be filed before *Kipling*.

16. D)

Married should be filed before *marvel*.

17. B)

Coffee should be filed before *Cooper*.

18. D)

Divert should be filed before *divest*.

19. D)

Tulip should be filed before *turntable*.

20. B)

Linger should be filed before *lipstick*.

21. D)

Patter should be filed before *Pavel*.

22. C)

Ribbit should be filed before *ribcage*.

23. D)

Consolidation should be filed before *continent*.

24. A)

Dubai should be filed before *dubbing*.

25. D)

Address should be filed before *adductor*.

26. A)

Xavier should precede all the names. The correctly alphabetized list would look like this: ***Xavier, Glenna; Xenos, Stavros; Xerox Corporation; Xiao, David***.

27. D)

Richardson should come after all the names. The correctly alphabetized list would look like this: ***Ricardo, Rhonda; Richard, Joyce; Richards, Sunny; Richardson, Leila***.

28. D)

The correctly alphabetized list would look like this: ***Thompkins, Rodney; Thompson, Wanda; Thomson, Yolanda; Tomkins, V.***

29. A)

Use the first word of the name to alphabetize companies. When two people share a surname, alphabetize by the first letter of the first name. If the first letter of the first name is the same, move to the second letter of the first name. The correctly alphabetized list would look like this: ***American Airlines Corp.; Armey, J.; Armstrong, James; Armstrong, Jonathan.***

30. D)

The correctly alphabetized list would look like this: ***Chalmers, Delshawn; Chamberlain, Alexia; Chambers, Lisa; Cho, Kim.***

31. D)

Businesses whose names begin with a number are alphabetized according to how the number would be written out. *95th* spells out to *ninety-fifth*, so it precedes *Mickey Norhill* and *Oliver Norris*. The correctly alphabetized list would look like this: ***Nguyen, Brandi; 95th Street Block Assn.; Norhill, Mickey; Norris, Oliver.***

32. B)

Because both *Tanya* and *Thomas* share the same surname (*Vickers*), use the first names to alphabetize. *Tanya* precedes *Thomas* according to the rules of alphabetization. The correctly alphabetized list would look like this: ***Velazquez, T.; Vickers, Tanya; Vickers, Thomas; Vickey, Torrey.***

33. B)

According to the rules of alphabetization, treat prefixes like *Mc* as part of the word. The correctly alphabetized list would look like this: ***Maloney, Sarah; McLellan, Ilana; McNally, David; Mendez, Mike.***

34. A)

To alphabetize hyphenated names, imagine the hyphen joins the two parts into one word. So *Gordon-Jackson* would follow *Gordon*. The correctly alphabetized list would look like this: ***Gordon, L.; Gordon-Jackson, Doug; Gosselin, Carlos; Grimwald, Kitty.***

35. D)

According to the rules of alphabetization, treat prefixes like *O'* as if they are part of the word (ignore the apostrophe). The correctly alphabetized list would look like this: ***Olivares,***

Joey; Oliver, Ryan; Orange, Rodney; O'Sullivan, Jordan.

36. B)

When last names and first initials are the same, the name with the initial precedes the name with the full first name. So *Jackie Ronaldo* comes after *J. Ronaldo*. The correctly alphabetized list would look like this: ***Ronaldo, J.; Ronaldo, Jackie; Rosenstein, Jerry; Ross, Jermaine.***

37. B)

The correctly alphabetized list would look like this: ***Green, L.; Greenberg, F.L.; Gu, Han F.; Gunnerson, Courtney F.***

38. D)

Articles like *the* are disregarded for the purposes of filing, so *The Microsoft Corp.* follows *Lakshmi R. Malkin*. The correctly alphabetized list would look like this: ***Malkin, Lakshmi R.; The Microsoft Corporation; Mitchell, Amy; Munoz, Roger.***

39. C)

T.J. Maxx is considered one name because it is the name of a company, so it comes first by way of the initial *T*. Articles like *the* are disregarded for the purposes of filing, so *The Target Company* precedes *Shawn Y. Taylor*. The correctly alphabetized list would look like this: ***T.J. Maxx, Inc.; The Target Company; Taylor, Shawn Y.; Tesla, Inc.***

40. A)

The correctly alphabetized list would look like this: ***Apple, Inc.; Appleton, Larry R.; Archer Farms, Inc.; Axios Technologies, LLC.***

41. A)

The correctly alphabetized list would look like this: ***Galligan, Karen; Gorman, K.; Gorman, Kim; Grimes, Kyle.***

42. C)

When individuals share a surname, the name without a middle initial precedes the name with one. The name with a middle initial precedes the name with a middle name that begins with the same letter. When last names and first initials are the same, the name with the initial precedes the name with the full first name. The correctly alphabetized list would look like this: ***Morales, J.P., Morales, Julianna; Morales, Julianna P.; Morales, Julianna Perez.***

43. C)

The correctly alphabetized list would look like this: ***Watkins, J.R.; Wilkins, Jerry; Williamson, V.; Wu, Vincent.***

44. A)

Use the first word of the name to alphabetize companies. The correctly alphabetized list would look like this: ***The Galley Group; Garrison, Jamal R.; Graystar Management, LLC; Greenwich, Tobias.***

45. C)

Use the first word of the name to alphabetize companies. The correctly alphabetized list would look like this: ***Forrest-Waller, Sam; Fortis Healthcare Ltd.; Foster, Carly R.; Future Retail Ltd.***

46. D)

Articles are considered part of the surname. According to the rules of alphabetization, treat prefixes like *D'* as if they are part of the word (ignore the apostrophe). The correctly alphabetized list would look like this: ***de la Vega, Delilah; Delgado, P.T.; Derringer, B. Thomas; D'Souza, Andrea.***

47. A)

Use the first word of the name to alphabetize companies. The correctly alphabetized list would look like this: ***Waxworth, Ophelia L.; Whitman, O.L.; Whittaker, Casey; Worthington Industries, LLC.***

48. B)

Articles are considered part of the surname. When two individuals share a surname, use their first names to determine who comes first in alphabetical order. The correctly alphabetized list would look like this: ***Lagrange, D.B.; La Grange, Ellen; Lefkowitz, Lois; Lockwood, Amelia R.***

49. D)

Use the first word of the name to alphabetize companies. Articles like *the* should be ignored when alphabetizing company names. When two individuals share a surname, use their first names to determine who comes first in alphabetical order. The correctly alphabetized list would look like this: ***The Glickman Photography Co.; Gorsky, Doris; Gorsky, J.B.; Granby, Jasmine.***

50. C)

Articles are considered part of the surname. The correctly alphabetized list would look like this: ***El Hajj, Ahmed; Elkins, Wilson E.; Elkinson, R.V.; Engels, Victoria.***

51. C)

When two individuals share a surname, use their first names to determine who comes first in alphabetical order. The correctly alphabetized list would look like this: ***Hernandez, Mike; Hernandez, Portia; Hidalgo, Van; Hill, Jennifer N.***

52. D)

When individuals share a surname, use their first names to determine who comes first in alphabetical order. If they also share first names, use the middle initial to alphabetize. The name without a middle initial precedes the name with one. The correctly alphabetized list would look like this: ***Colbert, Lawrence; Colbert, Lawrence N.; Colbert, Quentin T.; Colbert, R.N.***

53. D)

Use the first word of the name to alphabetize companies. The correctly alphabetized list would look like this: ***Heisenberg, Thayer E.; Heisenweiss, T.L.; Hellman, Tyrone E.; Hess Petroleum Co.***

54. B)

When individuals share a surname and a first name, the name without a middle initial precedes the name with one. The correctly alphabetized list would look like this: ***Burroughs, Kiana S.; Burroughs, William R.; Burrows, Julian; Burrows, Julian R.***

55. B)

When individuals share a surname, use their first names to determine who comes first in alphabetical order. If they also share first names, use the middle initial to alphabetize. The name with a middle initial precedes the name with a middle name that begins with the same letter. The correctly alphabetized list would look like this: ***Longview, Giuliana; Longview, Juliana P.; Longview, Richard J.; Longview, Richard Jackson.***

Filing Names

1. **C)**

   Both *Alexander* and *Alyssa* share the same last name, *Bryant. Alexander* should precede *Alyssa*.

2. **D)**

   Jillian, Alexander, and *Jonathan* share the same last name, *Worthington. Jillian* should precede *Jonathan* and follow *Alexander*.

3. **B)**

   Daniel and *Derek* share the same last name, *Lee. Daniel* should precede *Derek*.

4. **D)**

   Jennifer and *Whitney* share the same last name, *Rodriguez. Jennifer* should precede *Whitney*.

5. **B)**

   Jimmy and *Monica* share the same last name, *Watkins. Jimmy* should precede *Monica*.

6. **A)**

   Charles and *Rodney* share the same last name, *Wan. Charles* should precede *Rodney*.

7. **A)**

   Margaret and *Matthew* share the same last name, *Appelbaum. Margaret* should precede *Matthew*.

8. **C)**

   Rosie and *Goldie* share the same last name, *Jenkins. Rosie* should follow *Goldie*.

9. **B)**

   Ahmed and *Brian* share the same last name, *Jackson. Ahmed* should precede *Brian*.

10. **D)**

    Mary Beth and *Abagail* share the same last name, *Shapiro. Mary Beth* should follow *Abagail*.

11. **C)**

    Lachlan and *Elliot* share the same last name, *McEnaney. Lachlan* should follow *Elliot*.

12. **B)**

    Muhammad and *Fatima* share the same last name, *Haji. Muhammad* should follow *Fatima*.

13. **C)**

    Eugene and *Evgeni* share the same last name, *Ivanov. Eugene* should precede *Evgeni*.

14. **E)**

    Judith and *Edward* share the same last name, *Goldstein. Judith* should follow *Edward*.

15. **D)**

    Tiana and *Roland* share the same last name, *Hill. Tiana* should follow *Roland*.

16. **B)**

    Wilma and *Holly* share the same last name, *Martin. Wilma* should follow *Holly*.

17. **E)**

    Michael and *Hilda* share the same last name, *Carter. Michael* should follow *Hilda*.

18. **D)**

    Josiah and *Aramecia* share the same last name, *Mitchell. Josiah* should follow *Aramecia*.

19. **C)**

    Sarah and *Susanna* share the same last name, *Wright. Sarah* should precede *Susanna*.

20. **A)**

    Bryan and *Elijah* share the same last name, *Ackerman. Bryan* should precede *Elijah*.

21. **A)**

    Hershel and *Stephen* share the same last name, *Weismann. Hershel* should precede *Stephen*.

22. **D)**

    Matilda and *Destiny* share the same last name, *Taylor. Matilda* should follow *Destiny*.

23. **E)**

    Tiffany and *Jordan* share the same last name, *Fullerman. Tiffany* should follow *Jordan*.

24. D)

Jasmine and *Jesus* share the same last name, *Lopez*. *Jasmine* should precede *Jesus*.

25. C)

Malik, *Hailey*, and *Justin* all share the same last name, *Moore*. *Malik* should follow *Justin*.

Communication and Judgment

1. C)

The citizen is merely asking whether the curfew applies to neighborhood people walking their dogs. She (and every other citizen) should receive courteous treatment from the police. However, it's best not to make an exception in the case of a temporary curfew that has been put in place for the sake of public safety.

2. A)

The administrative assistant should start by asking for help from someone who works in human resources. Maybe if the supervisor is warned that it's inappropriate to keep asking for dates and that such behavior could result in his dismissal, he will stop. However, if the behavior continues, or if the organization has no human resources department, the administrative assistant will need to inform someone else, perhaps a different supervisor or a coworker who is higher up in the organization than the administrative assistant. The bottom line is that the supervisor's behavior is definitely inappropriate and could be cause for dismissal.

3. A)

First, the clerical worker should find out what the office rules are when it comes to substituting for others when they take vacation time. In most workplaces, employees must ask in advance to take their vacation time. By agreeing to substitute for a coworker if she can take over his duties, the clerical worker is building goodwill with her coworker. However, their supervisor needs to know about the arrangement in advance and must decide if it is workable.

4. C)

A gas leak could cause an explosion and needs to be addressed right away. The inspector needs to immediately call the fire department and/or the utility company to shut off the gas and investigate the leak. The other three situations may need attention too, but they are not emergencies and can wait until the gas leak is dealt with.

5. C)

The two clerical workers should start by asking their coworker whether he is aware that their task is a shared one and that he has not been doing as much of it as each of them has been doing. It is possible that their coworker needs more training or is unaware that his work habits are creating an unfair situation. If the situation continues, then the two clerical workers should involve the supervisor.

6. D)

The toll collector should start by asking her supervisor to provide high-quality protective gear like gloves, medical-grade face masks, and face shields. Public employees should not have to risk their lives (and their family's lives) to perform a necessary job. If the supervisor does not remedy the situation, the toll collector might call the county health department and find out what they recommend. If the toll collector belongs to a union, she might ask it for help, or she can contact the human resources department of the agency she works for.

7. C)

In order to search a driver and search their vehicle, an officer should have probable cause for the search. In this case, the officer believes that the driver was driving under the influence of alcohol—the probable cause is the erratic driving coupled with the smell of alcohol on the driver's breath. A "hunch" is not probable cause. Neither is a messy car—many law-abiding citizens have messy vehicles.

8. B)

If the mail carrier suspects that a physical assault is occurring, she should notify the police immediately. The other situations may eventually need attention, too, but they are not necessarily emergencies.

9. D)

The administrative assistant should start by telling his supervisor that he has heard her criticisms, and he wishes to do better. Maybe the supervisor is unaware of her overly strict, critical management style. It is probably not best to involve coworkers unless or until the assistant is very sure that he is being unfairly singled out for harsh treatment. Maybe he needs additional training or clarification to do a better job.

10. A)

A priority assignment is just that—a priority for the organization. You should help your coworker complete the priority assignment. Your own routine assignment can be put off for a little while.

11. D)

A police officer is not a firefighter. If he suspects that there is a fire, he should call the fire department before doing anything else. The fire department is responsible for taking care of this emergency situation. By trying to take charge of the situation himself (when he does not possess the requisite training), the officer may create a delay that endangers people's lives and causes more property damage.

12. C)

The supervisor should start by clearly but constructively explaining to the clerical assistant how his shortcomings have affected her. Then she should ask him what he thinks. Maybe he needs more training. Maybe the two of them just don't work well together, and he could do better on a different team. Maybe he simply isn't well suited to the position. The supervisor should clearly outline her expectations for improvement. If the situation does not improve, the assistant may need to be transferred or even terminated.

13. B)

The custodian should start by investigating the situation to see if it can be remedied in a simple, inexpensive way. If it cannot, he should speak to his supervisor about next steps, since they might be more expensive. The custodian should give the clerical worker the benefit of the doubt and trust that he would not complain if there were not an actual problem.

14. C)

The supervisor should have proof before accusing anyone of stealing. In the meantime, keeping valuables locked up (or out of the office altogether) is an acceptable temporary solution.

15. B)

The key words here are "often" and "occasionally." Occasional annoying or unusual behavior may be tolerated in the workplace. Some people even have disabilities that inhibit their behavioral skills, but they are still able to function appropriately in the workplace and carry out their duties. However, someone who often flies into rages is frightening to work with at the very least. In a worst-case scenario, he may become physically violent with coworkers.

16. A)

Three things: 1) clerical work is all about details; 2) different workers—including bosses—have different work styles; 3) this person is your boss, so within reason, you need to do things his way.

17. B)

In this situation, putting the inmate in handcuffs could prevent him from badly injuring himself. The other situations need solutions too, but handcuffing would not necessarily solve them.

18. D)

It probably means little or nothing that the two coworkers have excluded the assistant from their plans. Perhaps they have known each other longer than she has known them. It is unprofessional to become too wrapped up emotionally with coworkers. The assistant should rely on her own friends and family members outside of work.

19. B)

The downed electrical wire is the only one of these situations that requires immediate attention, as it could injure or even kill someone. The other situations may need to be addressed, but none of them poses an emergency.

20. C)

In an emergency situation like this one, the first priority is to save the patient's life. As long as the ambulance driver does not endanger the parade marchers, it is all right for the police officer to use her own judgment in this situation despite her supervisor's command.

Comparison Questions

1. **D)**
   All four names are different.

2. **B)**
   Two of the addresses are exactly alike.

3. **D)**
   All four names are different.

4. **A)**
   All four addresses are exactly alike.

5. **C)**
   Three of the names are exactly alike.

6. **A)**
   All four of the addresses are exactly alike.

7. **D)**
   All four names are different.

8. **B)**
   Two of the addresses are exactly alike.

9. **B)**
   Two of the names are exactly alike.

10. **D)**
    All four addresses are different.

11. **C)**
    Three of the names are exactly alike.

12. **C)**
    Three of the addresses are exactly alike.

13. **A)**
    All four names are exactly alike.

14. **B)**
    Two of the addresses are exactly alike.

15. **C)**
    Three of the names are exactly alike.

16. **A)**
    All three of the sets have mistakes.

17. **C)**
    One of the sets has a mistake.

18. **C)**
    One of the sets has a mistake.

19. **A)**
    All three of the sets have mistakes.

20. **B)**
    Two of the sets have mistakes.

21. **A)**
    All three of the sets have mistakes.

22. **D)**
    There are no mistakes in any of the sets.

23. **B)**
    Two of the sets have mistakes.

24. **D)**
    There are no mistakes in any of the sets.

25. **B)**
    Two of the sets have mistakes.

26. **A)**
    All three of the sets have mistakes.

27. **D)**
    There are no mistakes in any of the sets.

28. **D)**
    There are no mistakes in any of the sets.

29. **B)**
    Two of the sets have mistakes.

30. **A)**
    All three of the sets have mistakes.

Coding Questions

1. **A)**
    All three sets are correct.

2. **D)**
    None of the sets is matched correctly.

3. **D)**
    None of the sets is matched correctly.

4. **B)**
    Two of the sets are matched correctly.

5. **C)**
    One of the sets is matched correctly.

6. **C)**
    One of the sets is matched correctly.

7. **C)**
    One of the sets is matched correctly.

8. **B)**
    Two of the sets are matched correctly.

9. **A)**
    All three sets are correct.

10. **C)**
    One of the sets is matched correctly.

11. **B)**
    Two of the sets are matched correctly.

12. **C)**
    One of the sets is matched correctly.

13. **A)**
    All three sets are correct.

14. **A)**
    All three sets are correct.

15. **D)**
    None of the sets is matched correctly.

16. **D)**
    None of the sets is matched correctly.

17. **A)**
    All three sets are correct.

18. **B)**
    Two of the sets are matched correctly.

19. **C)**
    One of the sets is matched correctly.

20. **C)**
    One of the sets is matched correctly.

Memorization Questions

1. **B)**
    The suspect is wearing jeans and a hooded sweatshirt.

2. **D)**
    The subject is leaning against a squad car as one police officer frisks him.

3. **C)**
    The female police officer is holding onto handcuffs with her left hand.

4. **D)**
    There is a person (wearing black) lying on the ground in the upper-left-hand corner of the photograph.

5. **B)**
    The officer is placing a marker labeled with the number *2* near the crime scene.

6. **B)**
    There is one person lying on the ground in the upper-left-hand corner of the photo and there is also one officer.

7. **C)**

   The person in the photograph has a brush in their right hand.

8. **B)**

   There are two markers visible in the dirt.

9. **C)**

   The log, dirt, and plants most likely are part of a wooded area.

10. **C)**

    The handcuffs on the suspect indicate that the officer on the left is most likely detaining the suspect.

11. **C)**

    There is a traffic cone visible to the left of the suspect, through the officer's legs.

12. **C)**

    The suspect's face cannot be seen because it's facing away from the camera. It's not turned to the left or right.

13. **D)**

    The back of the officer's vest says *NYPD*.

14. **A)**

    The car's front-end is pointing to the left of the photo, indicating that it's most likely driving from right to left.

15. **C)**

    The officer is standing at an intersection, close to a crosswalk, indicating that he is likely directing traffic. The officer also has a traffic vest and gloves on.

Printed in Great Britain
by Amazon

67570049R00088